ELECTRIC SMOKER COOKBOK

Unleash the Potential of Your Electric Smoker

with 250 Beginner-Friendly Recipes!

Tips & Tricks for Epic BBQ

Johnny Wood

TABLE OF CONTENTS

CHAPTER 8: CHEESE AND NUTS RECIPES

CHAPTER 1: ELECTRIC SMOKING BASICS

Electric smoking has revolutionized the way we prepare and savor delicious smoked foods. With its convenience and ease of use, electric smokers have become increasingly popular among both seasoned pitmasters and beginners. In this chapter, we will delve into the fundamentals of electric smoking, exploring its benefits, equipment selection, essential tools, and safety guidelines.

The art of smoking food has a rich history, dating back centuries when our ancestors discovered the tantalizing flavors and tender textures that smoking imparted to meats, fish, and other ingredients. Traditionally, smoking involved the use of wood or charcoal smokers, which required constant monitoring, temperature adjustment, and tending to the fire. While these methods still hold a special place in the hearts of many barbecue enthusiasts, electric smokers have emerged as a convenient alternative, offering precise temperature control and hassle-free operation.

One of the key advantages of electric smokers is their ease of use. Unlike their traditional counterparts, electric smokers eliminate the need for constantly tending to a fire. They are equipped with electric heating elements that provide consistent and reliable heat, allowing you to set the desired temperature and focus on other tasks while your food smokes to perfection. This convenience makes electric smokers an excellent choice for those who want to enjoy the flavors of smoked food without the time-consuming process of managing a fire.

When it comes to choosing the right electric smoker, several factors should be considered. Size is an important consideration, as it determines the capacity of the smoker and how much food you can smoke at once. Consider the amount of space you have available and the number of people you plan to cook for. Additionally, pay attention to the construction quality of the smoker to ensure durability and heat retention. Temperature range is another crucial aspect to consider, as different recipes may require specific temperature settings. Some electric smokers also come with additional features like built-in meat probes or Bluetooth connectivity for remote monitoring.

Properly preparing your electric smoker is crucial to ensure optimal performance and results. This includes cleaning the smoker thoroughly before use and seasoning it to create a non-stick surface and enhance flavor. Familiarize yourself with the various components of your electric smoker, such as the heating element, water pan, and smoke box, understanding how they work together to create the perfect smoking environment.

As with any cooking method, safety should be a top priority when using an electric smoker. Always read and follow the manufacturer's instructions and safety guidelines. Ensure that your electric smoker is placed on a stable and heat-resistant surface, away from flammable materials. Never leave the smoker unattended while it's in operation, and keep a fire extinguisher nearby, just in case. It's also important to maintain proper ventilation to prevent the buildup of smoke and gases.

BENEFITS OF USING AN ELECTRIC SMOKER

Electric Smokers have become increasingly trendy over recent years - rightfully so since they effectively serve both knowledgeable pitmasters as well as novices. Hence, we will emphasize how an Electric Smoker can improve its user's overall smoking experience along with exploring some noteworthy benefits it offers compared to its older brothers; charcoal-wood ones.

Undoubtedly one significant benefit of electric smokers is their *simplicity of usage*. Avail yourself of hassle-free smoking with the push of a button, setting up your preferred temperature. Providing relief to individuals who either lack experience or time for tending to their smoker with fuel sources in need of constant supervision and modification.

Moreover, electric Smokers also cater to temperature-control enthusiasts, ensuring precise temperature maintenance throughout the smoking process, achieving *uniform cooking* within desired doneness yet ensuring flavor. What's more, setting and maintaining specific temperatures give you greater control over your final dish's consistency.

It doesn't end there; Electric smokers cater to those challenged at time-management as it renders itself a *timesaver* compared to traditional counterparts. Additionally, since they omit lengthy preheating issues; users can jump-start smoking sessions quicker covering unexpected guests or parties with more smoked food needs.

Finally *versatility* is key within electric smokers- experimenting with different recipes and smoking techniques is doable when catering a range of food selections such as meats, poultry items or fish – meaning vegetarians aren't left out either! As diversity within menu options allows for all-around culinary experimentation while meeting various tastes and dietary preferences smoothly. Electric smokers are unique in that they can be used both indoors and outdoors. Unlike traditional smokers, which typically require outdoor use due to the potential smoke and fumes electric smokers offer unparalleled flexibility. Regardless of the weather conditions you can set up your electric smoker in your backyard, patio, or even in a well ventilated kitchen. With this adaptability comes the added convenience of being suitable for individuals who live in apartments, condos, or areas with strict outdoor smoking restrictions.

Additionally electric smokers require *minimal maintenance* compared to other types of smokers. Without ashes or charcoal to clean up the process is significantly simplified. Removable racks and drip pans make cleaning the interior easy after each use. The low amount of residue and grease build up reduces overall maintenance requirements.

In terms of safety concerns when compared to traditional smokers electric models provide significant benefits because they lack open flames - resulting in reduced risk of flare ups or accidental fires. Automatic shut off timers and temperature controls add another layer of security.

Finally *consistent results* are easily achieved with electric smokers since precise temperature control ensures that your food cooks evenly every time you smoke it for optimal smokiness levels.

With an electric smokers reliability in delivering consistent results every time used make it worth the investment compared to other types of smokers that use charcoal or wood fuel sources. Electric smokers are well known for their energy efficiency that minimizes energy consumption while providing sufficient heat for smoking food without any environmental footprint. They also save costs by consuming less electricity than other types of cooking appliances.

Some traditionalists may argue that electric smokers fail to deliver depth in smoky flavor but modern electric smokers offer many options such as adding wood chips or pellets to enhance the flavor profile of smoked dishes. The "set it and forget it" convenience allows people stepping away from handling cooking tasks after placing desired temperature settings with their dish inside the appliance giving them enough time for other chores before they return to enjoy their delicious meal. Electric Smokers require minimum maintenance while delivering precision temperature control making them beginner friendly tools most people new to smoking techniques can efficiently operate; giving beginners an opportunity to learn without getting overwhelmed by using traditional smokers.

CHOOSING THE RIGHT ELECTRIC SMOKER

Electric smokers come in many types, shapes, sizes and offer an array of features synonymous with different brands today. To help streamline choices when selecting the right one here are some vital considerations:

Size and capacity - Because of how much food you desire smoked simultaneously keep in mind the size of your smoker's cooking space along with its overall size to make use most efficient while respecting spatial limitations.

Construction quality - durability is determined by construction material strength's ability to facilitate heat retention even under challenging outdoor conditions such as high temperatures; we recommend heavy-duty durable materials like stainless steel when making our selection.
Temperature Range: Versatility is key since different recipes require different temperature settings; therefore, choosing an electric smoker suiting these specific needs improve experience longevity greatly- opt for models that can maintain selected temperatures reliably

Additional features: differing functionalities come accompanied by improving smoking experiences like digital control panels, built-in meat probes aiding internal temperature monitoring; timers aiding cooking durations precision among others; identify useful functionalities vs frivolous ones that reflect your preferred features.

Portability – Allow the opportunity to enjoy smoking on camping trips, outdoor events by investing in a lightweight model equipped with user-friendly handles or wheels helping enhance portability while also providing features reflecting the quality product chosen. Portable electric smokers offer you the flexibility and convenience of smoking your food wherever you go.

However it's important to consider various factors when selecting an electric smoker so that you can have the best smoking experience. One such factor to bear in mind is ease of cleaning since smoking can leave behind residue and drippings. Therefore look for models with removable racks, drip pans, easy access ash or grease trays, non stick surfaces or porcelain coated interiors as these features make cleaning a breeze. Another factor to consider is budget. Electric smokers come in different price ranges based on their features build quality and brand reputation. Therefore set a budget range that works for you and look for a smoker that offers the best value for your investment. However ensure you balance your budget with the desired features and quality to avoid overspending. Moreover before making your final decision on which electric smoker to purchase its wise to read customer reviews and consider the reputation of the brand or model you have in mind. This will give you valuable insights into the performance, durability and overall satisfaction of previous buyers who have used similar models in dealing with their specific smoking needs.

By taking into consideration various aspects such as size and capacity construction quality temperature range additional features portability ease of cleaning budget customer reviews amongst others. then comparing different models before selecting an electric smoker that aligns with your preferences and culinary aspirations -you will encounter an interesting flavorful journey filled with delicious meats, fish or vegetables all smoked to perfection!

ESSENTIAL TOOLS AND ACCESSORIES

For those who enjoy using an electric smoker there are certain tools and accessories that are necessary for a successful cooking experience. Not only do these items make the process easier they also allow for optimal results when smoking meats. In this section we will discuss the essential tools and accessories needed for using an electric smoker with confidence.

One of the most important tools is a **reliable meat thermometer**. This key item allows you to monitor the internal temperature of your smoked meats accurately which is especially important given that different types of meat require specific temperature levels to ensure optimal doneness. Another essential item when smoking foods on an electric smoker is **wood chips or pellets** for infusing those delightful smoky flavors into whatever is being cooked! Most commonly used woods includes hickory, apple, mesquite, cherry or oak with different flavor intensities thus providing the opportunity experiment with various wood flavors until finding personal favorite combinations!

Drip pans serve their purpose by catching drippings from food preventing flare ups caused by hot fat while reducing hot spots; hence contributing greater efficiency during cleanup making it vastly simpler. **Long handled tongs** made from sturdy heat resistant materials offer not only safer handling but adequate reach required when moving delicate fish or large cuts of meat simply leaving you less worrying about burns or sacrificing tenderness due mishandling of any nature throughout process!

Finally **heat resistant gloves** contribute massively toward keeping hands protected from potential burning injuries while operating an electric smoker helping focus more so on optimizing on achieving culinary feats in style

Overall including these must have tools and accessories as part of your electric smoking set up will lead to tastier smoked meals each time whilst promoting safety awareness around this fabulous technique. When handling hot grates, pans, or tools while smoking your food - gloves made of high-quality heat-resistant materials should be used- ones that permit dexterity for handling the food and equipment effectively.

To enhance flavor/moisture as well as give an attractive coating- choose basting brushes with heat-resistant bristles and comfortable handles against your smoked foods' surface textures.

Aluminum foil serves various purposes as creating smoke packets for adding more flavor to the foods; and wrapping meats provides optimum conditions retaining moisture expanding flavors when required for even cooking.

To maintain your electric smoker's longevity - using **sturdy bristle-grill brushes** helps experience optimal performances by removing accumulated grease, residues aiding in maintaining non-stick grates preventing unwanted taste while smoking them.

A fruitful misting of water or fruit juice combinations during the smoking process from spray bottles keeps food surfaces moist preventing them from getting dried out enhanced flavors preventing any accidental flare-ups during smoking period providing adequate solutions magnifying perfect tastes!

Optimum protection is crucial against natural elements like rain/snow/dust/UV rays prolonging your electric smoker's lifespan. For this purpose, investing in a high-quality smoker cover is essential, ensuring it's ready for the next smoking session.

Although electric smokers are safer then traditional smokers always keeping a fire extinguisher nearby increases safety measures. Having a recipe book or smoking guide on hand can offer you invaluable inspiration and guidance when it comes to experimenting with new flavors smoking techniques and new smoked dishes for family, friends or guests. Expand your range by following recipes tailored to electric smokers designed to make this process smooth sailing.

SAFETY GUIDELINES FOR ELECTRIC SMOKING

Electric smokers are user friendly devices that offer convenience in outdoor cooking; however, ensuring safety measures while using them is essential for optimum results without accidents. To achieve this goal when using your electric smoker there are some crucial tips you need to adhere to:

1. Carefully read the manufacturer's instructions before use; follow specific recommendations highlighted in the manual relevant only for your model of an electric smoker regarding its usage precautions and operations.

2. To ensure a safe smoking experience, it's important to constantly monitor your electric smoker and ensure that it's functioning correctly.

3. Make use of protective gear such as heat resistant gloves and aprons to minimize the risk of accidental burns or exposure to hot surfaces. And remember - children and pets should always be kept at a safe distance from the smoker while it's in operation.

4. When opening your smoker to check or remove food take caution as steam, hot air and smoke may escape. To prevent burns or inhaling hot smoke stand back and allow excess heat or smoke to dissipate before fully opening the smoker. Additionally keep a fire extinguisher nearby in case of any emergencies.

5. Lastly following proper food safety guidelines is crucial for a successful smoking experience. Always use fresh ingredients and avoid expired or spoiled ones. And don't forget to regularly clean and sanitize all utensils cutting boards and surfaces that come into contact with raw or smoked food. Safe and hygienic food preparation requires taking certain measures including practicing good hand hygiene i.e regularly washing your hands thoroughly with soap and water before AND after handling any kind of food product.

It's essential to keep raw meats separate from other ingredients so cross-contamination doesn't occur which can be done via using designated cutting boards, utensils as appropriate when handling different raw vs cooked ingredients during meal prep activities. Marinading foods should ideally happen within the refrigerator rather than at room temperature since this strategy helps inhibit unhealthy bacteria-related growth issues.

Cooking takes focus since it's important for food products reach their recommended internal temperatures preferably checked through a meat thermometer before serving.

Promptly refrigerate or consume what remains once cooked e.g leftovers since doing so helps minimize bacterial flourishing risks overall. In addition, perishable foods left out at room temperature need disposal beyond two hours passed from initial preparation time (such as in an outdoor barbecue setting).

Remember that prioritizing safety protects not just from potential hazards it helps create an enjoyable worry-free environment promoting better overall meal satisfaction levels too during your electric smoking experience. Practice care in observing basic precautions like these guidelines and embark on your journey of electric smoking with confidence creating delicious and memorable smoked dishes guests will simply relish.

CHAPTER 2: TECHNIQUES & MAINTENANCE

Smoking is an incredibly versatile cooking technique that can impart unique and delicious flavors to a wide range of ingredients. In this chapter we'll explore three main smoking techniques: hot smoking, cold smoking, and combination smoking. By understanding these techniques you'll be able to elevate your electric smoking skills and create a variety of flavorful dishes.

Hot Smoking:

Hot smoking involves cooking food at higher temperatures between 200°F (93°C) and 275°F (135°C) while also infusing it with smoke. This is the most common method used for smoking food. Hot smoking is perfect for meats, poultry, fish, vegetables, and more! It produces a rich smoky flavor while also fully cooking the food which results in tender, moist, and fully flavored dishes. Furthermore, the higher temperatures used in hot smoking help to create a caramelized exterior for enhanced flavor and appearance. To ensure your food reaches a safe level of doneness use a meat thermometer to monitor the internal temperature during cooking. Cooking time will vary depending on the size and type of food being smoked.

Cold Smoking:

Unlike hot smoking which simultaneously cooks the food with heat generated by an electric smoker while producing smoke cold smoking primarily infuses food with smoke without applying heat for cooking. As such it is ideal for sensitive foods such as cheese cured meats fish or fruits that are delicate or sensitive to heat. Cold Smoking occurs at temperatures below 100°F (38C°) significantly lower than Hot Smoking. This method takes longer than other methods because it requires several hours or even days depending on how smoky you want your dish.

Despite lengthy curing times involved in Cold Smoking technique can impart phenomenal subtle smoky flavors while preserving texture/aesthetic delicacy in some ingredients.

Combination Smoking:

Combination Smoking utilizes both Cold & Hot Smocking Techniques in harmony thus combining their benefits on same dish- cold smoking adds a subtle smoky flavor and texture while hot smoking cooks and infuses the food with rich smoke. This technique is ideal for those who want to achieve a more complex flavor profile leaving them craving more of this signature taste. An electric smoker provides a fantastic option when considering cold smoking methods in reducing cooking temperatures while still delivering delicious smoky food.

Typically separating the heat source from the chamber through a connecting tube or pipe ensures precise control over resulting temperatures vital in achieving successful outcomes in terms of both safety and flavor depth - Proper airflow and ventilation being critical considerations throughout this process.

Preparing ingredients correctly before incorporating them into a smoker is essential as you will not be cooking them whatsoever- making it necessary that they are appropriately cured or pre-cooked before use. Combining both hot and cold techniques achieve maximum flavor concentration with tenderness simultaneously; this method provides fantastic outcomes when working with larger cuts of meat along with other tougher ingredients requiring lengthened exposure times initially before incorporating higher low hose cooking towards completion.

As always, closely monitoring all internal temperatures during the transition from cold to hot smoke increases safety in achieving successful outcomes and a delicious final product.

MAINTENANCE AND CARE OF ELECTRIC SMOKERS

To fully optimize smoking techniques alongside investing in an Electric smoker you must master proper maintenance techniques. Routine maintenance is crucial to the smoker's longevity, safety and delectable food preparations from slow-smoked meats or cheese recipes.

Cleaning your electric smoker after each use is pivotal for your food's safety and its optimal functionality. Always make sure the smoker cools down completely before cleaning it up; take out detachable parts like racks, drip pan then wash with warm soapy water or manufacturer instructions. Use a damp cloth to wipe off any residue or debris on any internal surfaces of the electric smoker. These routine actions help prevent grease buildup that affects functionality.

The **heating element** is particularly significant in an electric smoker; always keep it free since a dirty one can potentially led to malfunctions. Consistently check your heating element for physical damages or wearing, being sure to clean gently using soft brush/cloth if necessary. A sanitized heating element ensures consistent heat distribution in your cooking which eliminates potential malfunctions of any kind.

The **proactive inspection of all parts** in an electric smoker such as seals, hinges, gaskets, and electrical connections are highly recommended regularly over time. Replace any worn-out/damaged parts without delay; carefully reviewing manufacturer's instructions booklets/consulting customer support hotline would guide you properly on correct replacement part installation procedures.
Protecting an Electric Smoker from environmental factors like rain/snow/dust/UV rays achieved by covering up using a cover specially designed for your model when not in use substantially extends its lifespan. After completing each smoking session ensure Electric Smoker has cooled down completely before covering up again promptly.

Proper storage best practices include storing appliances that are clean, dry, and safe against external factors by temporary safekeeping simply place preserving environment benefits into play. This reduces breakdowns over time due to environmental influences leading high economic costs induced by poor storage ways later. Make a point of cleaning up your electric smoker thoroughly once done using it. Ensure there aren't any wood chips or pellet remnants left over before storing it away according to stipulated storage requirements by manufacturers, keeping it free from various types of damage areas around seams through checks regularly performed on its electrical connections which check cords ensuring electrical outlets grounded securely without signs of frayed wires indicating wear.

If you come across any frayed cords that cause loose connections or suggest an absence of grounding, avoid taking chances and get help from qualified electricians or appliance manufacturers on fixing the wiring to ensure safety during usage.

Make sure to read through provided safety guidelines and operational instructions religiously, ensuring you follow set protocols as well as other usage tips unique to your electric smoker. Following these protocols guarantees a safe smoking experience and optimum product quality outcome.

Maintenance keeps appliances running smoothly by promoting longevity and maximizing performance. As such, taking care of your electric smoker will lead to delicious smoked meals derived from it for a long time!

WOOD CHIPS AND FLAVOR SELECTION

The choice of wood chips in electric smoking commonly determines flavorful and aromatic infusions in smoked dishes. Different types of wood offer unique flavors and intensities which provide opportunities for diverse culinary experiences. This section delves into various options of wood chips available offering insights towards selecting your preferred flavors suited for your electric smoking endeavors.

Numerous options are available when it comes to selecting types of wood chips with each having its unique characteristics. **Mesquite** is bold popularly used in grilling & smoking beef, poultry, & pork. However, this should only be used sparingly or combined with milder woods since overusing can cause it to become quite strong. For versatility, **hickory** remains a classic choice known for its strength coupled with sweetness that pairs gracefully well across different meat types such as beef, pork, poultry, and game creating savory smoky flavors reminiscent of traditional barbecue taste.

For fruity mild notes an alternative would be **applewood** providing elegance complementing very naturally different meat types such as pork, poultry, and seafood while **cherrywood** provides slightly sweet fruity profiles coupled also offering delicate pleasant smokiness perfect for taste balance turkey, chicken, or fish-based dishes along with enhancing visual appeal containing reddish tinges. When looking for a medium-strong smoky flavor options **oaks** remain balanced enough often being used in smoking meats like beef, lamb, and game, offering classic smoky taste complementing ingredients majestically. When it comes to choosing the right type of wood chip when smoking meat or barbecuing dishes the important elements are subtle but essential.

Alderwood chips work great when creating a mild smoky flavor that doesn't overpower seafood dishes such as salmon showcasing their delicate natural taste profile.

It's critical that certain trees are avoided as they may produce toxic substances or resin that can depreciate food quality taste and even release dangerous chemicals when burned. These include pine, spruce, cedar, oleander, yew, or laburnum. Opt for reputable vendors who offer high-quality wood chips thoughtfully tailored specifically for smoking purposes sourced from safe tree types only.

The choice of foods imparted with flavors ultimately comes down to personal preference after some experimentation with different woods tastes which vary between unique flavors and aromas produced on the palate allowing you lots of room for exploring variety by mixing up a variants cocktail blend until an individualized flavor profile can be found specifically meant to please your tastes buds which may come in handy during entertaining occasions.

Remember always select additives-free high-quality wood chips which are safe from harmful chemicals. The variety available is extensive - consider markets specializing in specialty items services or hosting online vendors or better yet contact local suppliers who deal primarily in fruit tree trimmings sources at times these local businesses proved more cost-effectively than other mainstream stores, and the products tend to be fresher too!

MANAGING SMOKE LEVELS TIPS

Electric smokers offer an easy and convenient way to enjoy thoroughly smoked meals without heavy additional equipment that traditional smokers may require; however, getting the desired flavor balance requires careful consideration when it comes to how much smoke is utilized during food preparation. When using an electric smoker follow our useful tips on how to manage smoke levels effectively:

1. Begin by paying close attention to where you place your wood chips as it will be influential in how much smoked flavor comes through:

    - Distribute wood chips evenly across either tray or smoke box for consistent levels of natural flavors within dishes cooked.
    - Avoid overcrowding within compartments since this can cause excess exposure leading towards unwanted smell/taste overload.
    - Adding smaller portions repeatedly throughout when smoking dishes versus a heavier one-time transference provides a more efficient process.

2. Avoid underwhelming or overpowering your meals by paying attention to how you set up the ventilation system within your electric smoker

    - Adjust dampers or vents as required to create better circulation throughout the smoker and prevent smoke build up that may be over drying food.
    - Always frequently monitor vent positions depending on what is being cooked. This gives better control over the smoky aroma generated, keeping it consistent without overpowering or underwhelming natural flavors.

3. Be aware of cooking temperatures and their impacts:

- Lower smoking temperatures produce intense smoke giving an alluring aroma. It may slow down your cooking time in exchange for this desirable flavor.
- Higher smoking temperatures may create less overall smoke yet keep desired flavors infused throughout your dishes

In summary understanding how each of these techniques helps manage smoke levels will lead the way towards getting perfect results from an electrical smoker readily while maintaining safe measures! When cooking with an electric smoker, its essential to know how to regulate the intensity of smoky flavors.

4. Consider implementing the following time management tips:

- Longer Smoking Time: To achieve more robust smoky flavors within reasonable limits extend your smoking time for improved absorption into food – but avoid going too long which can overpower other notes.
- Shorter Smoking Time: If you prefer milder smokey flavors or working delicately flavored ingredients into your recipe then reduce smoking duration accordingly.

5. Tasting periodically during smoking is recommended:

- Start Conservatively: Begin with a moderate amount of wood chips then gradually adjust it as needed until you finally get desired smokiness.
- Tasting During Smoking: Sampling periodic bites in between intervals will help determine just how strong or mild smoky flavor should be.

Maintain this awareness through practice observations when regulating smoke production in any recipe; it takes practice but improves sensory judgment ability over time helping create balanced results that truly complement different recipes.

MONITORING AND CONTROLLING TEMPERATURE

Consistent temperature management is a requisite aspect that needs attention while using an electric smoker. The regulation of temperatures determines how well-cooked meats turn out thereby affecting their moisture retention and texture. Follow these instructive tips mentioned below, allowing optimal control overheat generation while achieving definitive taste demands if used properly:

Tip 1: Use a Reliable Thermometer

For proper tracking of your smoker's temperatures as well as the meats being roasted inside them use two types of thermometers while cooking in an electrical smoking system. Smoker thermometer built-in inside the device as a helpful reference to know about cooking chamber temperatures or similar, while Meat thermometer in edible items helping detect the right internal temperature required to attain ideal doneness.

Tip 2: Preheat Your Smoker

Before loading up the smoker with meats, always preheat electric smokers first as per manufacturer's instructions. Reach your preferred heat levels for stable results before smoking in any editable.

Tip 3: Regulate Temperature Control

Electric smokers come designed with knobs generally used for controlling heating capacity when smoking meats. Temperature regulation through proper ventilation is vital in controlling heating within an electric smoker effectively. It's imperative to maintain an open vent throughout operation ensuring smoke remains dense enough while circulating evenly around your food only before leaving thus ensuring evenly flavored smoked meat properly finished at precise internal core temperatures without impurities. External factors such as weather, temperature and even wind play a crucial role in either enhancing your cooking experience or doing the opposite.

Maintain moisture levels by using a water pan that is often included with electric smokers -they also help distribute heat evenly to prevent dryness. Mastering this craft takes patience because each electric smoker is unique and differing factors like weather effects come into play while regulating temperature. Give some extra attention to monitoring the smoke throughout the process...you will soon get deliciously smoked produce every time!

CHAPTER 3: SMOKING TIME AND TEMPERATURE

To achieve delicious dishes that are perfectly smoked you must take into consideration the smoking time and temperature. It is essential to balance these two factors as they can greatly affect your ingredients' textures, ideal doneness and infused smoky flavors. This chapter will explore the importance of smoking time and temperature and provide basic guidelines for different types of ingredients.

Smoking time refers to how long your ingredients stay in the smoker and is influenced by factors such as the type of food cuts' size and thickness desired doneness level, and personal preference. The smoking duration directly affects the moisture content, tenderness, and smokiness degree in your dishes.

On the other hand, smoking temperature refers to the heat level maintained inside the smoker during cooking. It plays a crucial role in achieving proper cooking results and flavor development. Controlling smoking temperature enables you to achieve an ideal balance between foods internal doneness level and smokiness. For beef cuts like brisket thicknesses vary as well as levels of marbling or desired doneness which all affect cooking times. **Brisket** happens to be one of the most famous cuts for smoking; it benefits from low heat slow cooking between temperatures ranging between 225°F (107°C) to 250°F (121°C). Plan for roughly one hour per lb (2.2 lbs = 1 kilogram) or approximately 1.5 hours per kilogram.

When it comes to ribs like **pork ribs or beef ribs**; they require different timing ranges at different temperatures ranges also measured at around 225°F (107°C) requiring a cook time period between approximately 4 6 hours depending on their thickness checked with a bend or toothpick test for tenderized results.

Please take note that although these guidelines may serve as a starting point for various types of ingredients adjustments may be necessary according to specific recipes or personal preferences along with variations unique to each individual ingredient involved. Aiming for deliciously flavored dishes in addition with perfecting food safety guidelines is crucial when preparing smoked steaks that are medium rare or medium level. Smoking **steaks** for up to two hours would work fine as long as you maintain temperatures around 250°F (121 Celsius)-275 °F(135 Celsius).

When cooking poultry such as turkey and chicken food safety is incredibly important. Whole **chickens** can be smoked by keeping them in 250°F -275°F(121° C 135°C) temperatures and should reach an internal temperature of at least165°F(74°C) after a smoking time of around three to four hours depending on their size. Smoking **whole turkeys** will require setting the cooking temperature to225 °F-250°F(107°C 121°C) that requires around thirty minutes per lb.

If you're into seafood consider adding some smoky flavors by smoking them without making it dry. Smoking **fish fillets** for up to two hours would work best with temperatures between180 °F (82 Celsius)- 200 °F (93 Celsius). Keep monitoring the internal temperature until it reaches at least145°F(63°C). Shellfish won't require as much heating as others do so aim for twenty to thirty minutes when smoking **shrimp or scallops** in ideal temperatures like about225 °F. With **firm veggies** like bell peppers, zucchini, or eggplant, pleasing smoky flavors can be added quickly within only thirty to forty five minutes of being smoked with high ideal temperatures like225 °F-250 °F! For those who love fresh produce in their smoke dishes- smaller tender veg such as tomatoes or mushrooms require shorter sojourn times at low temperatures around ~180°F to 200°F.

To ensure a perfectly smoked and flavorsome dish monitoring the internal temperature with a meat thermometer is essential. This allows for accurate readings while following safety standards set out in general guidelines.

Remember that personal preference, recipe specifics, and other factors may require slight adjustments of smoking times/temperatures. With practice and experience you can balance tenderness, smokiness levels & texture of your dishes to make them true works of art. When it comes to achieving delicious cooking and flavor controlling smoking temperature is paramount. Doing so allows for the perfect balance between smoky goodness and the desired level of internal doneness. While every recipe may require slight adjustments depending on preferences here are some general guidelines for smoking different types of food.

The journey of achieving perfectly smoked meats doesn't end when you remove them from the electric smoker. Resting and slicing play crucial roles in ensuring that the flavors are locked in, the juices are distributed evenly, and the presentation is visually appealing. In this chapter, we will explore the importance of resting and provide tips for slicing smoked meats to maximize their taste and texture.

1. The Importance of Resting:

   Resting is a vital step in the cooking process that allows the meat to relax, the juices to redistribute, and the flavors to fully develop. During the smoking process, the heat causes the meat's juices to move towards the surface. Resting helps prevent the juices from immediately escaping when the meat is sliced, resulting in a more flavorful and succulent end product. Here's how to properly rest smoked meats:

   - Tent with foil: Once you remove the meat from the electric smoker, tent it loosely with foil. This helps retain the heat and creates a gentle environment for the juices to redistribute.
   - Let it rest: Allow the meat to rest undisturbed for about 10 to 20 minutes. Resting times may vary depending on the size and type of meat. Larger cuts, such as a whole brisket or pork shoulder, may require longer resting times.

2. The Art of Slicing:

   Properly slicing smoked meats is crucial to achieve the desired texture and presentation. Follow these tips for successful slicing:

   - Find the grain: Identify the direction of the grain in the meat before slicing. The grain refers to the natural muscle fibers that run through the meat. Slicing against the grain helps ensure tenderness by shortening the meat fibers.
   - Use a sharp knife: A sharp knife is essential for clean and precise slices. A dull knife can tear the meat and result in uneven cuts. Sharpen your knife before slicing, and consider using a long, thin slicing knife or a carving knife for larger cuts.
   - Slice with confidence: Apply gentle pressure and make smooth, even strokes as you slice through the meat. Avoid sawing or applying too much pressure, as this can compress the meat and affect its texture.
   - Thickness of slices: The thickness of the slices can vary depending on personal preference and the type of meat. Thinner slices are ideal for sandwiches and wraps, while thicker slices are suitable for serving as individual portions.

3. Serving and Presentation:

After slicing, arrange the smoked meats on a platter or serving dish. Pay attention to the visual presentation by ensuring the slices are neatly arranged and evenly spaced. You can garnish the platter with fresh herbs, citrus wedges, or other decorative elements to enhance the visual appeal.

4. Storing Leftover Meat:

If you have leftover smoked meat, proper storage is crucial to maintain its quality. Follow these guidelines:

- Cool the meat: Allow the sliced meat to cool completely before storing. This helps prevent moisture buildup and bacterial growth.
- Wrap and refrigerate: Wrap the sliced meat tightly in plastic wrap or place it in airtight containers. Store it in the refrigerator for up to 3 to 4 days.
- Freezing: If you don't plan to consume the smoked meat within a few days, consider freezing it for longer-term storage. Wrap the slices individually in plastic wrap and place them in freezer bags. Properly stored, smoked meats can last in the freezer for up to 3 months.

Remember, resting and slicing are essential steps in the smoking process that contribute to the overall quality and enjoyment of your smoked meats. Taking the time to rest the meat allows the flavors to develop, while proper slicing ensures tender and visually appealing slices. Practice these techniques to elevate your smoked meat experience!

CHAPTER 4: BEEF RECIPES

Smokey Garlic Rosemary Beef Roast
Ingredients:
4-lb beef roast, 4 cloves of garlic (minced), 2 tbsp fresh rosemary (chopped), 1 tbsp olive oil, 1 tsp salt, 1/2 tsp black pepper.
Directions:
Preheat the electric smoker to 225°F (107°C). Rub the beef roast with olive oil, minced garlic, chopped rosemary, salt, and black pepper. Place the roast in the smoker and smoke for 4-6 hours, or until the internal temperature reaches 135°F (57°C) for medium-rare. Remove from the smoker and let it rest for 15 minutes before slicing.

Honey Mustard Glazed Smoked Beef Ribs
Ingredients:
3 lbs beef back ribs, 1/4 cup Dijon mustard, 2 tbsp honey, 1 tbsp apple cider vinegar, 1 tsp paprika, 1/2 tsp garlic powder, 1/2 tsp salt, 1/4 tsp black pepper.
Directions:
Preheat the electric smoker to 250°F (121°C). In a bowl, whisk together Dijon mustard, honey, apple cider vinegar, paprika, garlic powder, salt, and black pepper. Brush the mixture over the beef ribs. Place the ribs in the smoker and smoke for 4-5 hours, or until the meat is tender and the internal temperature reaches 190°F (88°C). Let the ribs rest for 10 minutes before serving.

Teriyaki Pineapple Beef Skewers
Ingredients:
2 lbs beef sirloin (cut into 1-inch cubes), 1 cup teriyaki sauce, 1/2 cup pineapple juice, 2 tbsp brown sugar, 2 cloves garlic (minced), 1 tsp grated fresh ginger, 1 red bell pepper (cut into chunks), 1 green bell pepper (cut into chunks), 1 red onion (cut into chunks).
Directions:
Preheat the electric smoker to 275°F (135°C). In a bowl, combine teriyaki sauce, pineapple juice, brown sugar, minced garlic, and grated ginger. Thread beef cubes, bell peppers, and red onion onto skewers. Brush the teriyaki marinade over the skewers. Place the skewers in the smoker and smoke for 30-40 minutes, or until the beef is cooked to your desired doneness. Serve hot.

Smoked Beef Stuffed Bell Peppers
Ingredients:
4 large bell peppers (any color), 1 lb ground beef, 1 cup cooked rice, 1/2 cup diced tomatoes, 1/2 cup shredded cheddar cheese, 1/4 cup diced onion, 1/4 cup diced celery, 1 clove garlic (minced), 1 tsp dried oregano, 1/2 tsp salt, 1/4 tsp black pepper.
Directions:
Preheat the electric smoker to 275°F (135°C). Cut off the tops of the bell peppers and remove the seeds. In a skillet, cook the ground beef until browned. Drain any excess fat. Add cooked rice, diced tomatoes, shredded cheddar cheese, diced onion, diced celery, minced garlic, dried oregano, salt, and black

pepper to the skillet. Stir to combine. Stuff the bell peppers with the beef mixture. Place the stuffed peppers in the smoker and smoke for 1-2 hours, or until the peppers are tender. Serve hot.

Smokey BBQ Beef Sliders
Ingredients:
1 lb ground beef, 1/2 cup BBQ sauce, 1/4 cup bread crumbs, 1/4 cup diced onion, 1 clove garlic (minced), 1 tsp smoked paprika, 1/2 tsp salt, 1/4 tsp black pepper, Slider buns, Pickles, BBQ sauce (for serving).
Directions:
Preheat the electric smoker to 275°F (135°C). In a bowl, combine ground beef, BBQ sauce, bread crumbs, diced onion, minced garlic, smoked paprika, salt, and black pepper. Mix well. Form the mixture into small patties. Place the patties in the smoker and smoke for 1-1.5 hours, or until the internal temperature reaches 160°F (71°C). Toast the slider buns on the smoker for a few minutes. Assemble the sliders with the beef patties, pickles, and additional BBQ sauce. Serve warm.

Smoked Beef Chili
Ingredients:
2 lbs beef chuck roast (cubed), 1 can kidney beans (drained and rinsed), 1 can diced tomatoes, 1 cup beef broth, 1 onion (diced), 2 cloves garlic (minced), 2 tbsp chili powder, 1 tbsp ground cumin, 1 tbsp smoked paprika, 1 tsp oregano, 1/2 tsp salt, 1/4 tsp black pepper.
Directions:
Preheat the electric smoker to 250°F (121°C). In a large pot, combine beef chuck roast, kidney beans, diced tomatoes, beef broth, diced onion, minced garlic, chili powder, ground cumin, smoked paprika, oregano, salt, and black pepper. Stir well. Place the pot in the smoker and smoke for 4-6 hours, or until the beef is tender. Stir occasionally. Serve hot with your favorite chili toppings.

Smoked Beef Fajitas
Ingredients:
1.5 lbs beef flank steak, 1 red bell pepper (diced), 1 green bell pepper (diced), 1 yellow bell pepper (diced), 1 onion (sliced), 2 cloves garlic (minced), 2 tbsp olive oil, 1 tbsp chili powder, 1 tsp ground cumin, 1 tsp paprika, 1/2 tsp salt, 1/4 tsp black pepper, Flour tortillas, Salsa, Guacamole, Sour cream (for serving).
Directions:
Preheat the electric smoker to 275°F (135°C). In a bowl, combine diced red, green, and yellow bell peppers, sliced onion, minced garlic, olive oil, chili powder, ground cumin, paprika, salt, and black pepper. Toss to coat the vegetables. Place the marinated vegetables in a disposable aluminum foil pan. Place the flank steak on top of the vegetables. Place the pan in the smoker and smoke for 2-3 hours, or until the beef reaches your desired level of doneness. Remove the steak from the pan and let it rest for 10 minutes. Slice the steak against the grain. Warm the flour tortillas on the smoker. Assemble the fajitas by filling the tortillas with sliced beef and smoked vegetables. Serve with salsa, guacamole, and sour cream.

Smoked Beef Bruschetta
Ingredients:

1 baguette, 1 lb beef tenderloin, 1 tbsp olive oil, 1 tsp dried thyme, 1 tsp garlic powder, 1/2 tsp salt, 1/4 tsp black pepper, 1 cup diced tomatoes, 1/4 cup chopped fresh basil, 2 tbsp balsamic vinegar, 1 clove garlic (minced), 1/4 tsp salt, 1/4 tsp black pepper, Fresh mozzarella cheese (sliced).

Directions:

Preheat the electric smoker to 275°F (135°C). Slice the baguette into 1-inch thick slices. Brush the slices with olive oil and place them on a baking sheet. In a small bowl, combine dried thyme, garlic powder, salt, and black pepper. Rub the beef tenderloin with the spice mixture. Place the beef tenderloin in the smoker and smoke for 1-2 hours, or until the internal temperature reaches 135°F (57°C) for medium-rare. Remove the beef from the smoker and let it rest for 10 minutes. Meanwhile, in a bowl, combine diced tomatoes, chopped basil, balsamic vinegar, minced garlic, salt, and black pepper. Mix well. To assemble the bruschetta, place a slice of smoked beef on each baguette slice. Top with the tomato mixture and a slice of fresh mozzarella cheese. Place the bruschetta back in the smoker for a few minutes, until the cheese melts. Serve warm.

Smoked Beef Stir-Fry

Ingredients:

1.5 lbs beef sirloin (thinly sliced), 2 tbsp soy sauce, 2 tbsp hoisin sauce, 1 tbsp rice vinegar, 1 tbsp honey, 2 cloves garlic (minced), 1 tsp grated fresh ginger, 1/2 tsp Chinese five-spice powder, 1/4 tsp red pepper flakes, 2 tbsp vegetable oil, 1 onion (sliced), 2 bell peppers (sliced), 1 cup sliced mushrooms, 1 cup snap peas, Cooked rice (for serving).

Directions:

Preheat the electric smoker to 275°F (135°C). In a bowl, whisk together soy sauce, hoisin sauce, rice vinegar, honey, minced garlic, grated ginger, Chinese five-spice powder, and red pepper flakes. Add the sliced beef to the marinade and let it sit for 15-20 minutes. In a large skillet or wok, heat vegetable oil over medium-high heat. Add the sliced onion, bell peppers, mushrooms, and snap peas. Stir-fry for 5-7 minutes, until the vegetables are tender-crisp. Remove the vegetables from the skillet and set aside. In the same skillet, add the marinated beef and cook for 3-4 minutes, until browned and cooked through. Add the stir-fried vegetables back to the skillet and toss to combine. Serve the smoked beef stir-fry over cooked rice.

Smoked Beef and Vegetable Kabobs

Ingredients:

1.5 lbs beef sirloin (cut into 1-inch cubes), 1 red bell pepper (cut into chunks), 1 yellow bell pepper (cut into chunks), 1 zucchini (sliced), 1 red onion (cut into chunks), 1 cup cherry tomatoes, 2 tbsp olive oil, 2 cloves garlic (minced), 1 tsp dried thyme, 1 tsp dried rosemary, 1/2 tsp salt, 1/4 tsp black pepper.

Directions:

Preheat the electric smoker to 275°F (135°C). In a bowl, combine olive oil, minced garlic, dried thyme, dried rosemary, salt, and black pepper. Add the beef cubes to the bowl and toss to coat evenly. Thread the marinated beef cubes, bell pepper chunks, zucchini slices, red onion chunks, and cherry tomatoes onto skewers. Place the skewers in the smoker and smoke for 1-1.5 hours, or until the beef is cooked to your desired doneness and the vegetables are tender. Serve hot.

Smoked Beef Quesadillas

Ingredients:

1 lb beef skirt steak, 1 tbsp olive oil, 1 tsp chili powder, 1 tsp ground cumin, 1/2 tsp garlic powder, 1/2 tsp salt, 1/4 tsp black pepper, 4 large flour tortillas, 2 cups shredded Monterey Jack cheese, Sliced jalapenos (optional), Sour cream (for serving), Salsa (for serving).
Directions:
Preheat the electric smoker to 275°F (135°C). Rub the beef skirt steak with olive oil, chili powder, ground cumin, garlic powder, salt, and black pepper. Place the steak in the smoker and smoke for 1-2 hours, or until the internal temperature reaches your desired level of doneness. Remove the steak from the smoker and let it rest for 10 minutes. Slice the steak into thin strips. Heat a large skillet over medium heat. Place a tortilla in the skillet and sprinkle with shredded Monterey Jack cheese. Top with sliced beef and jalapenos if desired. Place another tortilla on top. Cook for 2-3 minutes, then flip and cook for an additional 2-3 minutes until the cheese is melted and the tortillas are crispy. Repeat with the remaining tortillas and filling. Cut the quesadillas into wedges and serve with sour cream and salsa.

Smoked Beef and Broccoli
Ingredients:
1.5 lbs beef sirloin (sliced), 3 cups broccoli florets, 1 onion (sliced), 2 cloves garlic (minced), 1/4 cup soy sauce, 2 tbsp oyster sauce, 1 tbsp brown sugar, 1 tsp grated fresh ginger, 1/2 tsp cornstarch, 1/4 tsp red pepper flakes, 1 tbsp vegetable oil.
Directions:
Preheat the electric smoker to 275°F (135°C). In a small bowl, whisk together soy sauce, oyster sauce, brown sugar, grated ginger, cornstarch, and red pepper flakes. Set aside. Heat vegetable oil in a skillet or wok over high heat. Add sliced beef and stir-fry for 2-3 minutes, until browned. Remove the beef from the skillet and set aside. In the same skillet, add sliced onion and minced garlic. Stir-fry for 2 minutes until fragrant. Add broccoli florets and continue stir-frying for 3-4 minutes until the broccoli is tender-crisp. Return the beef to the skillet and pour the sauce mixture over the beef and broccoli. Stir well to coat everything evenly. Cook for an additional 2-3 minutes until the sauce thickens. Serve hot over rice or noodles.

Smoked Beef and Cabbage Stir-Fry
Ingredients:
1.5 lbs beef sirloin (sliced), 4 cups shredded cabbage, 1 carrot (julienned), 1 red bell pepper (sliced), 1 onion (sliced), 2 cloves garlic (minced), 2 tbsp soy sauce, 1 tbsp oyster sauce, 1 tbsp hoisin sauce, 1 tsp sesame oil, 1/2 tsp cornstarch, 1/4 tsp red pepper flakes, 2 tbsp vegetable oil.
Directions:
Preheat the electric smoker to 275°F (135°C). In a small bowl, whisk together soy sauce, oyster sauce, hoisin sauce, sesame oil, cornstarch, and red pepper flakes. Set aside. Heat vegetable oil in a skillet or wok over high heat. Add sliced beef and stir-fry for 2-3 minutes, until browned. Remove the beef from the skillet and set aside. In the same skillet, add sliced onion and minced garlic. Stir-fry for 2 minutes until fragrant. Add shredded cabbage, julienned carrot, and sliced red bell pepper. Continue stir-frying for 4-5 minutes until the vegetables are tender-crisp. Return the beef to the skillet and pour the sauce mixture over the beef and vegetables. Stir well to coat everything evenly. Cook for an additional 2-3 minutes until the sauce thickens. Serve hot over rice or noodles.

Smoked Beef and Mushroom Stroganoff
Ingredients:

1.5 lbs beef sirloin (sliced), 8 oz sliced mushrooms, 1 onion (sliced), 2 cloves garlic (minced), 1 cup beef broth, 1 cup sour cream, 2 tbsp all-purpose flour, 1 tbsp Worcestershire sauce, 1 tbsp Dijon mustard, 1 tsp dried thyme, 1/2 tsp salt, 1/4 tsp black pepper, Egg noodles (cooked, for serving), Chopped fresh parsley (for garnish).

Directions:

Preheat the electric smoker to 275°F (135°C). In a large skillet, heat some oil over medium-high heat. Add sliced beef and cook for 2-3 minutes until browned. Remove the beef from the skillet and set aside. In the same skillet, add sliced onion and minced garlic. Cook for 2 minutes until fragrant. Add sliced mushrooms and cook for an additional 4-5 minutes until the mushrooms are tender. In a small bowl, whisk together beef broth, sour cream, all-purpose flour, Worcestershire sauce, Dijon mustard, dried thyme, salt, and black pepper. Pour the sauce mixture into the skillet with the mushrooms and onions. Stir well to combine. Return the beef to the skillet and simmer for 5-7 minutes until the sauce thickens. Serve the smoked beef stroganoff over cooked egg noodles. Garnish with chopped fresh parsley.

Smoked Beef Lettuce Wraps

Ingredients:

1.5 lbs beef sirloin (thinly sliced), 1 tbsp soy sauce, 1 tbsp hoisin sauce, 1 tbsp rice vinegar, 1 tsp grated fresh ginger, 1 clove garlic (minced), 1/2 tsp cornstarch, 1/4 tsp red pepper flakes, 1 tbsp vegetable oil, 1 onion (diced), 1 bell pepper (diced), 1 cup sliced mushrooms, Lettuce leaves (such as butter lettuce or romaine), Chopped green onions (for garnish), Chopped peanuts (for garnish).

Directions:

Preheat the electric smoker to 275°F (135°C). In a small bowl, whisk together soy sauce, hoisin sauce, rice vinegar, grated ginger, minced garlic, cornstarch, and red pepper flakes. Set aside. Heat vegetable oil in a skillet or wok over high heat. Add sliced beef and stir-fry for 2-3 minutes, until browned. Remove the beef from the skillet and set aside. In the same skillet, add diced onion, diced bell pepper, and sliced mushrooms. Stir-fry for 4-5 minutes until the vegetables are tender-crisp. Return the beef to the skillet and pour the sauce mixture over the beef and vegetables. Stir well to coat everything evenly. Cook for an additional 2-3 minutes until the sauce thickens. To serve, spoon the beef and vegetable mixture onto lettuce leaves. Garnish with chopped green onions and chopped peanuts. Roll up the lettuce leaves to form wraps and enjoy!

Smoked Beef and Cheese Stuffed Peppers

Ingredients:

1.5 lbs ground beef, 1 cup cooked rice, 1 cup shredded cheddar cheese, 1/2 cup diced tomatoes, 1/4 cup diced onion, 2 cloves garlic (minced), 2 tbsp chopped fresh parsley, 1 tsp chili powder, 1/2 tsp cumin, 1/2 tsp salt, 1/4 tsp black pepper, 4 large bell peppers (any color), 1/4 cup beef broth.

Directions:

Preheat the electric smoker to 275°F (135°C). In a bowl, mix ground beef, cooked rice, shredded cheddar cheese, diced tomatoes, diced onion, minced garlic, chopped fresh parsley, chili powder, cumin, salt, and black pepper. Cut the tops off the bell peppers and remove the seeds. Stuff each bell pepper with the beef mixture. Place the stuffed peppers in a baking dish and pour beef broth into the dish. Cover the dish with foil. Place the dish in the smoker and smoke for 2-3 hours, or until the peppers are tender and the internal temperature of the beef reaches 160°F (71°C). Remove the foil for the last 15 minutes of cooking to allow the cheese to melt and the tops to brown slightly. Serve hot.

Smoked Beef and Bacon-Wrapped Asparagus

Ingredients:

1.5 lbs beef tenderloin (cut into 1-inch cubes), 16-20 asparagus spears, 8-10 slices bacon, 2 tbsp olive oil, 1 tsp garlic powder, 1/2 tsp salt, 1/4 tsp black pepper.

Directions:

Preheat the electric smoker to 275°F (135°C). Wrap each beef cube with a slice of bacon and secure with a toothpick. Place the bacon-wrapped beef cubes on a baking sheet. In a small bowl, combine olive oil, garlic powder, salt, and black pepper. Brush the mixture onto the bacon-wrapped beef cubes. Arrange the asparagus spears on a separate baking sheet and drizzle with a little olive oil. Place both the beef cubes and asparagus in the smoker and smoke for 30-40 minutes, or until the beef is cooked to your desired level of doneness and the asparagus is tender. Remove the toothpicks from the beef cubes before serving. Serve the smoked beef and bacon-wrapped asparagus together as a delicious appetizer or main course.

Smoked Beef and Vegetable Skewers with Chimichurri Sauce

Ingredients:

1.5 lbs beef sirloin (cut into 1-inch cubes), 1 zucchini (sliced), 1 yellow bell pepper (cut into chunks), 1 red onion (cut into chunks), 1 cup cherry tomatoes, Wooden skewers (soaked in water), 1 cup fresh parsley (chopped), 1/4 cup fresh cilantro (chopped), 2 cloves garlic (minced), 1/4 cup red wine vinegar, 1/4 cup olive oil, 1/2 tsp dried oregano, 1/4 tsp red pepper flakes, 1/2 tsp salt, 1/4 tsp black pepper.

Directions:

Preheat the electric smoker to 275°F (135°C). Thread the beef cubes, zucchini slices, bell pepper chunks, onion chunks, and cherry tomatoes onto the wooden skewers, alternating the ingredients. In a blender or food processor, combine fresh parsley, fresh cilantro, minced garlic, red wine vinegar, olive oil, dried oregano, red pepper flakes, salt, and black pepper. Blend until smooth to make the chimichurri sauce. Place the skewers in the smoker and smoke for 20-30 minutes, or until the beef is cooked to your desired level of doneness and the vegetables are tender. Serve the smoked beef and vegetable skewers with the chimichurri sauce for dipping or drizzling.

Smoked Beef and Spinach Stuffed Mushrooms

Ingredients:

1.5 lbs ground beef, 16-20 large mushrooms (stems removed), 1 cup chopped spinach, 1/2 cup shredded mozzarella cheese, 1/4 cup grated Parmesan cheese, 2 cloves garlic (minced), 1 tsp dried oregano, 1/2 tsp salt, 1/4 tsp black pepper.

Directions:

Preheat the electric smoker to 275°F (135°C). In a large bowl, combine ground beef, chopped spinach, shredded mozzarella cheese, grated Parmesan cheese, minced garlic, dried oregano, salt, and black pepper. Mix until well combined. Stuff each mushroom cap with the beef and spinach mixture, pressing it gently into the cap. Place the stuffed mushrooms on a baking sheet or in a baking dish. Transfer the baking sheet or dish to the smoker and smoke for 30-40 minutes, or until the beef is cooked through and the mushrooms are tender. Remove from the smoker and let them cool slightly before serving.

Smoked Beef and Sweet Potato Hash

Ingredients:

1.5 lbs beef stew meat (cubed), 2 large sweet potatoes (peeled and cubed), 1 onion (diced), 2 cloves garlic (minced), 1 red bell pepper (diced), 1 green bell pepper (diced), 2 tbsp olive oil, 1 tsp smoked paprika, 1/2 tsp dried thyme, 1/2 tsp salt, 1/4 tsp black pepper.

Directions:

Preheat the electric smoker to 275°F (135°C). In a large bowl, toss together beef stew meat, cubed sweet potatoes, diced onion, minced garlic, diced red bell pepper, and diced green bell pepper. Drizzle with olive oil and sprinkle with smoked paprika, dried thyme, salt, and black pepper. Toss until well coated. Transfer the mixture to a baking dish or disposable aluminum foil pan. Place the dish or pan in the smoker and smoke for 2-3 hours, or until the beef is tender and the sweet potatoes are cooked through. Stir occasionally during the smoking process. Serve the smoked beef and sweet potato hash as a hearty and flavorful meal.

Smoked Beef and Mushroom Risotto

Ingredients:

1.5 lbs beef sirloin (thinly sliced), 2 cups Arborio rice, 8 cups beef broth, 1 cup sliced mushrooms, 1 onion (diced), 2 cloves garlic (minced), 1/2 cup grated Parmesan cheese, 2 tbsp butter, 2 tbsp olive oil, 1 tsp dried thyme, 1/2 tsp salt, 1/4 tsp black pepper.

Directions:

Preheat the electric smoker to 275°F (135°C). In a large skillet, heat butter and olive oil over medium heat. Add sliced beef and cook for 2-3 minutes until browned. Remove the beef from the skillet and set aside. In the same skillet, add diced onion and minced garlic. Cook for 2 minutes until fragrant. Add sliced mushrooms and cook for an additional 4-5 minutes until the mushrooms are tender. In a separate large pot, bring beef broth to a simmer. Add Arborio rice to the pot and cook according to package instructions, stirring occasionally. As the rice cooks, gradually add the simmering beef broth, about 1 cup at a time, stirring constantly until the liquid is absorbed before adding more. Continue this process until the rice is tender and creamy. Stir in the cooked beef, mushrooms, dried thyme, salt, and black pepper. Cook for an additional 2-3 minutes to heat through. Remove from heat and stir in the grated Parmesan cheese. Let the risotto rest for a few minutes before serving.

Smoked Beef and Tomato Pasta

Ingredients:

1.5 lbs beef stew meat (cubed), 8 oz pasta (your choice of type), 1 can diced tomatoes, 1 onion (diced), 2 cloves garlic (minced), 2 tbsp tomato paste, 1 tbsp olive oil, 1 tsp dried basil, 1/2 tsp dried oregano, 1/2 tsp salt, 1/4 tsp black pepper, Grated Parmesan cheese (for serving), Fresh basil leaves (for garnish).

Directions:

Preheat the electric smoker to 275°F (135°C). Cook the pasta according to package instructions until al dente. Drain and set aside. In a large skillet, heat olive oil over medium heat. Add beef stew meat and cook for 2-3 minutes until browned. Remove the beef from the skillet and set aside. In the same skillet, add diced onion and minced garlic. Cook for 2 minutes until fragrant. Add diced tomatoes, tomato paste, dried basil, dried oregano, salt, and black pepper. Stir well to combine. Return the beef to the skillet and mix with the tomato mixture. Transfer the beef and tomato mixture to a baking dish or disposable aluminum foil pan. Place the dish or pan in the smoker and smoke for 2-3 hours, or until the beef is tender and the flavors are well blended. Serve the smoked beef and tomato sauce over the cooked pasta. Sprinkle with grated Parmesan cheese and garnish with fresh basil leaves.

Smoked Beef and Barley Soup

Ingredients:

1.5 lbs beef chuck roast (cubed), 1 cup barley, 4 cups beef broth, 2 cups water, 1 onion (diced), 2 carrots (diced), 2 celery stalks (diced), 2 cloves garlic (minced), 1 tsp dried thyme, 1 bay leaf, 1/2 tsp salt, 1/4 tsp black pepper, Fresh parsley (for garnish).

Directions:

Preheat the electric smoker to 275°F (135°C). In a large pot, combine beef chuck roast, barley, beef broth, water, diced onion, diced carrots, diced celery, minced garlic, dried thyme, bay leaf, salt, and black pepper. Stir well. Place the pot in the smoker and smoke for 4-6 hours, or until the beef is tender and the barley is cooked through. Stir occasionally. Remove the bay leaf before serving. Serve the smoked beef and barley soup hot, garnished with fresh parsley.

Smoked Beef and Quinoa Stuffed Peppers

Ingredients:

1.5 lbs ground beef, 1 cup cooked quinoa, 4 large bell peppers (any color), 1 cup diced tomatoes, 1/2 cup diced onion, 2 cloves garlic (minced), 1 tsp dried basil, 1/2 tsp dried oregano, 1/2 tsp salt, 1/4 tsp black pepper, 1/2 cup shredded mozzarella cheese.

Directions:

Preheat the electric smoker to 275°F (135°C). In a bowl, combine ground beef, cooked quinoa, diced tomatoes, diced onion, minced garlic, dried basil, dried oregano, salt, and black pepper. Mix well. Cut off the tops of the bell peppers and remove the seeds. Stuff each bell pepper with the beef and quinoa mixture. Place the stuffed peppers in a baking dish. Transfer the dish to the smoker and smoke for 2-3 hours, or until the peppers are tender and the beef is cooked through. During the last 10 minutes of cooking, sprinkle shredded mozzarella cheese over the stuffed peppers and allow it to melt. Remove from the smoker and let them cool slightly before serving.

Smoked Beef and Chickpea Salad

Ingredients:

1.5 lbs beef sirloin (thinly sliced), 1 can chickpeas (drained and rinsed), 1 cucumber (diced), 1 red bell pepper (diced), 1/2 red onion (thinly sliced), 1/4 cup chopped fresh parsley, 2 tbsp lemon juice, 2 tbsp olive oil, 1 tsp ground cumin, 1/2 tsp paprika, 1/2 tsp salt, 1/4 tsp black pepper.

Directions:

Preheat the electric smoker to 275°F (135°C). In a bowl, combine sliced beef sirloin, chickpeas, diced cucumber, diced red bell pepper, thinly sliced red onion, chopped fresh parsley, lemon juice, olive oil, ground cumin, paprika, salt, and black pepper. Toss to combine well. Transfer the mixture to a disposable aluminum foil pan. Place the pan in the smoker and smoke for 1-2 hours, or until the beef is cooked to your desired level of doneness. Remove from the smoker and let it cool slightly before serving. Serve the smoked beef and chickpea salad as a refreshing and protein-packed meal.

Smoked Beef and Herb Stuffed Tomatoes

Ingredients:

1.5 lbs beef tenderloin (thinly sliced), 4 large tomatoes, 1/2 cup breadcrumbs, 1/4 cup grated Parmesan cheese, 2 tbsp chopped fresh basil, 2 tbsp chopped fresh parsley, 2 cloves garlic (minced), 2 tbsp olive oil, 1/2 tsp salt, 1/4 tsp black pepper.

Directions:

Preheat the electric smoker to 275°F (135°C). Cut off the tops of the tomatoes and scoop out the seeds and pulp. In a bowl, combine breadcrumbs, grated Parmesan cheese, chopped fresh basil, chopped fresh parsley, minced garlic, olive oil, salt, and black pepper. Mix well. Stuff each tomato with the bread crumb mixture. Place the stuffed tomatoes in a baking dish or on a baking sheet. Transfer the dish or sheet to the smoker and smoke for 1-2 hours, or until the tomatoes are softened and the flavors are infused. Remove from the smoker and let them cool slightly before serving. Serve the smoked beef and herb stuffed tomatoes as a delightful side dish or appetizer.

Smoked Beef and Avocado Wraps

Ingredients:

1.5 lbs beef sirloin (thinly sliced), 4 large tortilla wraps, 2 avocados (sliced), 1 cup shredded lettuce, 1/2 cup diced tomatoes, 1/4 cup sliced red onion, 2 tbsp lime juice, 2 tbsp mayonnaise, 1 tsp chili powder, 1/2 tsp cumin, 1/2 tsp garlic powder, 1/2 tsp salt, 1/4 tsp black pepper.

Directions:

Preheat the electric smoker to 275°F (135°C). In a small bowl, mix together mayonnaise, lime juice, chili powder, cumin, garlic powder, salt, and black pepper to make the sauce. Set aside. Place the beef slices in the smoker and smoke for 1-2 hours, or until cooked to your desired level of doneness. Remove from the smoker and let it cool slightly. Warm the tortilla wraps in a skillet or microwave. Spread a layer of the sauce onto each wrap. Top with smoked beef slices, sliced avocados, shredded lettuce, diced tomatoes, and sliced red onion. Roll up the wraps tightly and cut in half if desired. Serve the smoked beef and avocado wraps as a delicious and filling meal.

Smoked Beef and Blue Cheese Salad

Ingredients:

1.5 lbs beef tenderloin (thinly sliced), 4 cups mixed salad greens, 1 cup cherry tomatoes (halved), 1/2 cup crumbled blue cheese, 1/4 cup chopped walnuts, 2 tbsp balsamic vinegar, 2 tbsp olive oil, 1 tsp Dijon mustard, 1/2 tsp honey, 1/2 tsp salt, 1/4 tsp black pepper.

Directions:

Preheat the electric smoker to 275°F (135°C). Place the beef slices in the smoker and smoke for 1-2 hours, or until cooked to your desired level of doneness. Remove from the smoker and let it cool slightly. In a small bowl, whisk together balsamic vinegar, olive oil, Dijon mustard, honey, salt, and black pepper to make the dressing. Set aside. Arrange the mixed salad greens on a large serving platter. Top with cherry tomatoes, crumbled blue cheese, and chopped walnuts. Slice the smoked beef and place it over the salad. Drizzle the dressing over the salad or serve it on the side. Toss gently to combine all the ingredients. Serve the smoked beef and blue cheese salad as a flavorful and satisfying meal.

Smoked Beef and Caramelized Onion Pizza

Ingredients:

1.5 lbs beef sirloin (thinly sliced), 1 pizza dough (store-bought or homemade), 1 cup marinara sauce, 1 cup shredded mozzarella cheese, 1 cup caramelized onions, 1/4 cup sliced black olives, 2 tbsp olive oil, 1 tsp dried oregano, 1/2 tsp garlic powder, 1/2 tsp salt, 1/4 tsp black pepper.

Directions:

Preheat the electric smoker to 275°F (135°C). Place the beef slices in the smoker and smoke for 1-2 hours, or until cooked to your desired level of doneness. Remove from the smoker and let it cool slightly. Roll out the pizza dough on a floured surface to your desired thickness. Transfer the dough to a pizza stone or baking sheet. Spread marinara sauce evenly over the dough, leaving a border for the crust. Sprinkle shredded mozzarella cheese over the sauce. Top with smoked beef slices, caramelized onions, and sliced black olives. Drizzle olive oil over the pizza and sprinkle with dried oregano, garlic powder, salt, and black pepper. Place the pizza in the smoker and smoke for 20-30 minutes, or until the crust is golden brown and the cheese is melted and bubbly. Remove from the smoker and let it cool slightly before slicing. Serve the smoked beef and caramelized onion pizza as a delicious and unique twist on traditional pizza.

Smoked Beef and Eggplant Roll-Ups

Ingredients:

1.5 lbs beef sirloin (thinly sliced), 2 medium eggplants, 1 cup ricotta cheese, 1/4 cup grated Parmesan cheese, 2 tbsp chopped fresh basil, 2 tbsp chopped fresh parsley, 1 clove garlic (minced), 2 cups marinara sauce, 1/2 tsp dried oregano, 1/2 tsp salt, 1/4 tsp black pepper.

Directions:

Preheat the electric smoker to 275°F (135°C). Slice the eggplants lengthwise into thin strips. Place the eggplant slices on a baking sheet and sprinkle with salt. Let them sit for 10 minutes to draw out excess moisture. Rinse the eggplant slices and pat them dry with paper towels. In a bowl, combine ricotta cheese, grated Parmesan cheese, chopped fresh basil, chopped fresh parsley, and minced garlic. Mix well. Spread a spoonful of the ricotta mixture onto each eggplant slice. Place a slice of smoked beef on top of the ricotta mixture. Roll up the eggplant slice tightly and secure it with a toothpick. Repeat with the remaining eggplant slices, ricotta mixture, and smoked beef. Pour marinara sauce into a baking dish. Sprinkle dried oregano, salt, and black pepper over the sauce. Place the eggplant roll-ups in the dish, seam side down. Transfer the dish to the smoker and smoke for 1-2 hours, or until the eggplant is tender and the flavors are infused. Remove the toothpicks before serving. Serve the smoked beef and eggplant roll-ups with marinara sauce for dipping or drizzling.

Smoked Beef and Potato Hash Browns

Ingredients:

1.5 lbs beef sirloin (thinly sliced), 4 cups grated potatoes, 1 onion (diced), 2 cloves garlic (minced), 2 tbsp olive oil, 1 tsp smoked paprika, 1/2 tsp dried thyme, 1/2 tsp salt, 1/4 tsp black pepper, Chopped fresh parsley (for garnish), Fried eggs (optional, for serving).

Directions:

Preheat the electric smoker to 275°F (135°C). In a large skillet, heat olive oil over medium heat. Add diced onion and minced garlic. Cook for 2 minutes until fragrant. Add grated potatoes, smoked paprika, dried thyme, salt, and black pepper. Stir well to combine. Cook the potato mixture for 8-10 minutes, stirring occasionally, until the potatoes are golden brown and crispy. Remove the potato hash browns from the skillet and set aside. In the same skillet, add sliced beef and cook for 2-3 minutes until browned. Remove the beef from the skillet and let it cool slightly. Chop the smoked beef into small pieces. In a separate pan, fry the eggs, if desired. To serve, divide the potato hash browns onto plates. Top with chopped smoked beef and fried eggs, if using. Garnish with chopped fresh parsley. Enjoy the smoked beef and potato hash browns as a delicious and satisfying breakfast or brunch.

Smoked Beef and Zucchini Noodle Stir-Fry

Ingredients:

1.5 lbs beef sirloin (sliced), 4 medium zucchini (spiralized or cut into thin strips), 1 red bell pepper (sliced), 1 yellow bell pepper (sliced), 1 cup sliced mushrooms, 1/2 cup shredded carrots, 3 cloves garlic (minced), 2 tbsp soy sauce, 1 tbsp sesame oil, 1 tbsp honey, 1 tsp grated fresh ginger, 1/2 tsp red pepper flakes, 1/2 tsp salt, 1/4 tsp black pepper, 2 tbsp chopped green onions (for garnish), Sesame seeds (for garnish).

Directions:

Preheat the electric smoker to 275°F (135°C). In a small bowl, whisk together soy sauce, sesame oil, honey, grated ginger, red pepper flakes, salt, and black pepper. Set aside. Place the beef slices in the smoker and smoke for 1-2 hours, or until cooked to your desired level of doneness. Remove from the smoker and let it cool slightly. In a large skillet or wok, heat a tbsp of oil over medium-high heat. Add minced garlic and cook for 1 minute until fragrant. Add bell peppers, mushrooms, and shredded carrots. Stir-fry for 3-4 minutes until the vegetables are tender-crisp. Add the spiralized or thinly sliced zucchini to the skillet and cook for an additional 2-3 minutes until the zucchini is slightly softened. Pour the soy sauce mixture over the vegetables and stir well to coat. Add the smoked beef slices to the skillet and toss to combine everything. Cook for another 2-3 minutes to heat through. Remove from heat. Serve the smoked beef and zucchini noodle stir-fry hot, garnished with chopped green onions and sesame seeds.

Smoked Beef and Roasted Vegetable Wrap

Ingredients:

1.5 lbs beef sirloin (thinly sliced), 4 large tortilla wraps, 1 cup roasted red bell peppers (sliced), 1 cup roasted zucchini (sliced), 1 cup roasted eggplant (sliced), 1/2 cup crumbled feta cheese, 2 tbsp balsamic vinegar, 2 tbsp olive oil, 1 tsp dried oregano, 1/2 tsp garlic powder, 1/2 tsp salt, 1/4 tsp black pepper.

Directions:

Preheat the electric smoker to 275°F (135°C). Place the beef slices in the smoker and smoke for 1-2 hours, or until cooked to your desired level of doneness. Remove from the smoker and let it cool slightly. In a small bowl, whisk together balsamic vinegar, olive oil, dried oregano, garlic powder, salt, and black pepper to make the dressing. Set aside. Warm the tortilla wraps in a skillet or microwave. Spread a layer of the dressing onto each wrap. Top with smoked beef slices, roasted red bell peppers, roasted zucchini, roasted eggplant, and crumbled feta cheese. Roll up the wraps tightly and cut in half if desired. Serve the smoked beef and roasted vegetable wraps as a flavorful and satisfying meal.

Smoked Beef and Cabbage Stir-Fry

Ingredients:

1.5 lbs beef sirloin (thinly sliced), 4 cups shredded cabbage, 1 cup sliced carrots, 1 cup sliced bell peppers (any color), 1 cup sliced snow peas, 1/2 cup sliced green onions, 3 cloves garlic (minced), 2 tbsp soy sauce, 1 tbsp oyster sauce, 1 tbsp sesame oil, 1 tsp grated fresh ginger, 1/2 tsp red pepper flakes, 1/2 tsp salt, 1/4 tsp black pepper, Sesame seeds (for garnish).

Directions:

Preheat the electric smoker to 275°F (135°C). In a small bowl, whisk together soy sauce, oyster sauce, sesame oil, grated ginger, red pepper flakes, salt, and black pepper. Set aside. Place the beef slices in the smoker and smoke for 1-2 hours, or until cooked to your desired level of doneness. Remove from the smoker and let it cool slightly. In a large skillet or wok, heat a tbsp of oil over medium-high heat. Add minced garlic and cook for 1 minute until fragrant. Add sliced carrots, bell peppers, and snow peas. Stir-fry for 3-4 minutes until the vegetables are tender-crisp. Add shredded cabbage and sliced green onions to the skillet. Continue to stir-fry for another 2-3 minutes until the cabbage is slightly wilted. Pour the sauce over the vegetables and stir well to coat. Add the smoked beef slices to the skillet and toss to combine everything. Cook for another 2-3 minutes to heat through. Remove from heat. Serve the smoked beef and cabbage stir-fry hot, garnished with sesame seeds.

Smoked Beef and Mushroom Pot Pie

Ingredients:

1.5 lbs beef chuck roast (cubed), 2 cups sliced mushrooms, 1 onion (diced), 2 cloves garlic (minced), 2 tbsp butter, 2 tbsp all-purpose flour, 1 cup beef broth, 1/2 cup milk, 1 tsp dried thyme, 1/2 tsp dried rosemary, 1/2 tsp salt, 1/4 tsp black pepper, 1 package refrigerated pie crusts.

Directions:

Preheat the electric smoker to 275°F (135°C). In a large skillet, melt the butter over medium heat. Add diced onion and minced garlic. Cook for 2 minutes until fragrant. Add sliced mushrooms and cook for an additional 4-5 minutes until the mushrooms are tender. Add beef chuck roast to the skillet and cook until browned on all sides. Sprinkle flour over the meat and vegetables and stir well to coat. Cook for 1-2 minutes to cook out the raw flour taste. Gradually pour in the beef broth and milk, stirring constantly to prevent lumps. Add dried thyme, dried rosemary, salt, and black pepper. Stir well. Transfer the mixture to a baking dish. Roll out the refrigerated pie crusts and place one over the baking dish, trimming the edges. Cut a few slits on top to allow steam to escape. Place the pot pie in the smoker and smoke for 2-3 hours, or until the beef is tender and the crust is golden brown. Remove from the smoker and let it cool slightly before serving. Serve the smoked beef and mushroom pot pie as a comforting and flavorful meal.

Smoked Beef and Spinach Stuffed Portobello Mushrooms

Ingredients:

1.5 lbs beef sirloin (thinly sliced), 4 large Portobello mushrooms, 2 cups fresh spinach, 1 cup shredded mozzarella cheese, 1/4 cup grated Parmesan cheese, 2 cloves garlic (minced), 2 tbsp olive oil, 1 tsp dried oregano, 1/2 tsp dried basil, 1/2 tsp salt, 1/4 tsp black pepper.

Directions:

Preheat the electric smoker to 275°F (135°C). Remove the stems from the Portobello mushrooms and gently scrape out the gills. In a large skillet, heat olive oil over medium heat. Add minced garlic and cook for 1 minute until fragrant. Add fresh spinach to the skillet and cook until wilted. Remove from heat and let it cool slightly. In a bowl, combine wilted spinach, shredded mozzarella cheese, grated Parmesan cheese, dried oregano, dried basil, salt, and black pepper. Mix well. Fill each Portobello mushroom cap with the spinach and cheese mixture. Place the stuffed mushrooms on a baking sheet. Transfer the sheet to the smoker and smoke for 1-2 hours, or until the mushrooms are tender and the cheese is melted and bubbly. Remove from the smoker and let them cool slightly before serving. Serve the smoked beef and spinach stuffed Portobello mushrooms as a flavorful and satisfying appetizer or main dish.

CHAPETR 5: CHICHEK AND LAMB RECIPES

Smoked Lemon Pepper Chicken
Ingredients:
4 bone-in chicken breasts, 2 lemons (zested and juiced), 2 tbsp olive oil, 1 tbsp black pepper, 1 tsp salt, 1 tsp dried thyme.
Directions:
Preheat the electric smoker to 275°F (135°C). In a small bowl, combine lemon zest, lemon juice, olive oil, black pepper, salt, and dried thyme to make a marinade. Place the chicken breasts in a resealable bag and pour the marinade over them. Seal the bag and massage the marinade into the chicken. Let it marinate in the refrigerator for 1-2 hours. Remove the chicken from the marinade and discard the marinade. Place the chicken in the smoker and smoke for 1-2 hours, or until the internal temperature reaches 165°F (74°C). Remove from the smoker and let it rest for a few minutes before serving.

Smoked BBQ Chicken Drumsticks
Ingredients:
8 chicken drumsticks, 1 cup barbecue sauce, 2 tbsp brown sugar, 1 tbsp paprika, 1 tsp garlic powder, 1 tsp onion powder, 1/2 tsp salt, 1/4 tsp black pepper.
Directions:
Preheat the electric smoker to 275°F (135°C). In a small bowl, combine barbecue sauce, brown sugar, paprika, garlic powder, onion powder, salt, and black pepper to make a glaze. Place the chicken drumsticks in a baking dish and brush them with the glaze, reserving some for basting. Place the dish in the smoker and smoke for 2-3 hours, basting the drumsticks with the glaze every 30 minutes. Cook until the internal temperature reaches 165°F (74°C) and the chicken is cooked through and tender.

Smoked Teriyaki Chicken Skewers
Ingredients:
4 boneless, skinless chicken breasts (cut into 1-inch cubes), 1/2 cup soy sauce, 1/4 cup honey, 2 tbsp rice vinegar, 2 tbsp sesame oil, 2 cloves garlic (minced), 1 tsp grated fresh ginger, 1/2 tsp black pepper.
Directions:
Preheat the electric smoker to 275°F (135°C). In a bowl, whisk together soy sauce, honey, rice vinegar, sesame oil, minced garlic, grated ginger, and black pepper to make a marinade. Thread the chicken cubes onto skewers and place them in a shallow dish. Pour the marinade over the chicken skewers, reserving some for basting. Let them marinate in the refrigerator for 1-2 hours. Place the skewers in the smoker and smoke for 1-2 hours, basting with the reserved marinade every 30 minutes. Cook until the internal temperature reaches 165°F (74°C) and the chicken is tender and juicy.

Smoked Herb-Roasted Cornish Hens
Ingredients:
4 Cornish hens, 4 tbsp butter (melted), 2 tbsp chopped fresh rosemary, 2 tbsp chopped fresh thyme, 2 tbsp chopped fresh parsley, 2 cloves garlic (minced), 1 tsp salt, 1/2 tsp black pepper.
Directions:

Preheat the electric smoker to 275°F (135°C). In a small bowl, combine melted butter, chopped rosemary, chopped thyme, chopped parsley, minced garlic, salt, and black pepper to make a herb butter. Rub the herb butter all over the Cornish hens, including under the skin. Place the hens in the smoker and smoke for 2-3 hours, or until the internal temperature reaches 165°F (74°C) and the skin is golden brown and crispy. Remove from the smoker and let them rest for a few minutes before serving.

Smoked Maple-Glazed Chicken Thighs
Ingredients:
8 chicken thighs, 1/4 cup maple syrup, 2 tbsp Dijon mustard, 1 tbsp soy sauce, 1 tbsp apple cider vinegar, 1 tsp smoked paprika, 1/2 tsp garlic powder, 1/2 tsp onion powder, 1/2 tsp salt, 1/4 tsp black pepper.
Directions:
Preheat the electric smoker to 275°F (135°C). In a bowl, whisk together maple syrup, Dijon mustard, soy sauce, apple cider vinegar, smoked paprika, garlic powder, onion powder, salt, and black pepper to make a glaze. Place the chicken thighs in a baking dish and brush them with the glaze, reserving some for basting. Place the dish in the smoker and smoke for 2-3 hours, basting the thighs with the glaze every 30 minutes. Cook until the internal temperature reaches 165°F (74°C) and the chicken is cooked through and juicy.

Smoked Lemon Herb Turkey Breast
Ingredients:
1 bone-in turkey breast (about 6 lbs), 1 lemon (sliced), 4 sprigs fresh rosemary, 4 sprigs fresh thyme, 4 sprigs fresh sage, 4 cloves garlic (minced), 2 tbsp olive oil, 1 tsp salt, 1/2 tsp black pepper.
Directions:
Preheat the electric smoker to 275°F (135°C). Place the turkey breast on a large cutting board and pat it dry with paper towels. Using your fingers, carefully loosen the skin from the meat, being careful not to tear it. Insert lemon slices, fresh herbs, and minced garlic under the skin. Rub the turkey breast with olive oil, salt, and black pepper, ensuring even coverage. Place the turkey breast in the smoker and smoke for 4-5 hours, or until the internal temperature reaches 165°F (74°C) and the skin is golden brown and crisp. Remove from the smoker and let it rest for 20 minutes before carving.

Smoked Honey Mustard Chicken Wings
Ingredients:
2 lbs chicken wings, 1/4 cup honey, 2 tbsp Dijon mustard, 2 tbsp soy sauce, 1 tbsp apple cider vinegar, 1 tsp smoked paprika, 1/2 tsp garlic powder, 1/2 tsp onion powder, 1/2 tsp salt, 1/4 tsp black pepper.
Directions:
Preheat the electric smoker to 275°F (135°C). In a bowl, whisk together honey, Dijon mustard, soy sauce, apple cider vinegar, smoked paprika, garlic powder, onion powder, salt, and black pepper to make a marinade. Place the chicken wings in a resealable bag and pour the marinade over them. Seal the bag and massage the marinade into the wings. Let them marinate in the refrigerator for 1-2 hours. Remove the wings from the marinade and discard the marinade. Place the wings in the smoker and smoke for 2-3 hours, or until the internal temperature reaches 165°F (74°C) and the skin is crispy. Remove from the smoker and let them rest for a few minutes before serving.

Smoked Herbed Lamb Chops

Ingredients:

8 lamb chops, 2 tbsp olive oil, 2 cloves garlic (minced), 1 tbsp chopped fresh rosemary, 1 tbsp chopped fresh thyme, 1 tsp salt, 1/2 tsp black pepper.

Directions:

Preheat the electric smoker to 275°F (135°C). In a small bowl, combine olive oil, minced garlic, chopped rosemary, chopped thyme, salt, and black pepper to make a marinade. Rub the marinade all over the lamb chops, ensuring even coverage. Place the lamb chops in the smoker and smoke for 1-2 hours, or until the internal temperature reaches 145°F (63°C) for medium-rare. Adjust the cooking time according to your desired level of doneness. Remove from the smoker and let them rest for a few minutes before serving.

Smoked Lemon Garlic Whole Chicken

Ingredients:

1 whole chicken (about 4 lbs), 1 lemon (zested and juiced), 4 cloves garlic (minced), 2 tbsp olive oil, 1 tbsp chopped fresh rosemary, 1 tbsp chopped fresh thyme, 1 tsp salt, 1/2 tsp black pepper.

Directions:

Preheat the electric smoker to 275°F (135°C). In a small bowl, combine lemon zest, lemon juice, minced garlic, olive oil, chopped rosemary, chopped thyme, salt, and black pepper to make a marinade. Rub the marinade all over the whole chicken, including inside the cavity. Place the chicken in the smoker and smoke for 3-4 hours, or until the internal temperature reaches 165°F (74°C) in the thickest part of the thigh. Remove from the smoker and let it rest for 20 minutes before carving.

Smoked Moroccan Spiced Lamb Kebabs

Ingredients:

1.5 lbs lamb leg meat (cut into 1-inch cubes), 1 onion (diced), 2 cloves garlic (minced), 2 tbsp olive oil, 1 tbsp ground cumin, 1 tbsp ground coriander, 1 tbsp paprika, 1 tsp ground cinnamon, 1 tsp ground ginger, 1/2 tsp cayenne pepper, 1/2 tsp salt, 1/4 tsp black pepper.

Directions:

Preheat the electric smoker to 275°F (135°C). In a bowl, combine diced onion, minced garlic, olive oil, ground cumin, ground coriander, paprika, ground cinnamon, ground ginger, cayenne pepper, salt, and black pepper to make a marinade. Add the lamb cubes to the marinade and toss to coat them evenly. Let the lamb marinate in the refrigerator for 1-2 hours. Thread the marinated lamb cubes onto skewers. Place the skewers in the smoker and smoke for 2-3 hours, or until the internal temperature reaches 145°F (63°C) for medium-rare. Adjust the cooking time according to your desired level of doneness. Remove from the smoker and let them rest for a few minutes before serving.

Smoked Lemon Herb Turkey Legs

Ingredients:

4 turkey legs, 2 lemons (zested and juiced), 4 cloves garlic (minced), 2 tbsp olive oil, 1 tbsp chopped fresh rosemary, 1 tbsp chopped fresh thyme, 1 tsp salt, 1/2 tsp black pepper.

Directions:

Preheat the electric smoker to 275°F (135°C). In a small bowl, combine lemon zest, lemon juice, minced garlic, olive oil, chopped rosemary, chopped thyme, salt, and black pepper to make a marinade. Rub the marinade all over the turkey legs, ensuring even coverage. Place the turkey legs in the smoker and smoke for 3-4 hours, or until the internal temperature reaches 165°F (74°C) in the thickest part of the leg. Remove from the smoker and let them rest for a few minutes before serving.

Smoked Honey Mustard Glazed Chicken Breast

Ingredients: 4 chicken breasts, 1/4 cup honey, 2 tbsp Dijon mustard, 2 tbsp soy sauce, 1 tbsp apple cider vinegar, 1 tsp smoked paprika, 1/2 tsp garlic powder, 1/2 tsp onion powder, 1/2 tsp salt, 1/4 tsp black pepper.

Directions: Preheat the electric smoker to 275°F (135°C). In a bowl, whisk together honey, Dijon mustard, soy sauce, apple cider vinegar, smoked paprika, garlic powder, onion powder, salt, and black pepper to make a glaze. Place the chicken breasts in a baking dish and brush them with the glaze, reserving some for basting. Place the dish in the smoker and smoke for 2-3 hours, basting the breasts with the glaze every 30 minutes. Cook until the internal temperature reaches 165°F (74°C) and the chicken is cooked through and juicy.

Smoked Garlic Rosemary Cornish Game Hens

Ingredients:
4 Cornish game hens, 4 cloves garlic (minced), 2 tbsp chopped fresh rosemary, 2 tbsp olive oil, 1 tsp salt, 1/2 tsp black pepper.

Directions:
Preheat the electric smoker to 275°F (135°C). In a small bowl, combine minced garlic, chopped rosemary, olive oil, salt, and black pepper to make a marinade. Rub the marinade all over the Cornish game hens, including under the skin. Place the hens in the smoker and smoke for 2-3 hours, or until the internal temperature reaches 165°F (74°C) and the skin is golden brown and crispy. Remove from the smoker and let them rest for a few minutes before serving.

Smoked Lemon Herb Roasted Chicken

Ingredients:
1 whole chicken (about 4 lbs), 1 lemon (sliced), 4 sprigs fresh rosemary, 4 sprigs fresh thyme, 4 cloves garlic (minced), 2 tbsp olive oil, 1 tsp salt, 1/2 tsp black pepper.

Directions:
Preheat the electric smoker to 275°F (135°C). Place the whole chicken on a large cutting board and pat it dry with paper towels. Using your fingers, carefully loosen the skin from the meat, being careful not to tear it. Insert lemon slices, fresh herbs, and minced garlic under the skin. Rub the chicken with olive oil, salt, and black pepper, ensuring even coverage. Place the chicken in the smoker and smoke for 3-4 hours, or until the internal temperature reaches 165°F (74°C) in the thickest part of the thigh. Remove from the smoker and let it rest for 20 minutes before carving.

Smoked Balsamic Glazed Turkey Drumsticks

Ingredients:
4 turkey drumsticks, 1/2 cup balsamic vinegar, 1/4 cup honey, 2 tbsp soy sauce, 2 cloves garlic (minced), 1 tsp dried thyme, 1/2 tsp smoked paprika, 1/2 tsp salt, 1/4 tsp black pepper.

Directions:
Preheat the electric smoker to 275°F (135°C). In a small saucepan, combine balsamic vinegar, honey, soy sauce, minced garlic, dried thyme, smoked paprika, salt, and black pepper. Cook over medium heat, stirring occasionally, until the glaze thickens slightly. Place the turkey drumsticks in a baking dish and brush them with the glaze, reserving some for basting. Place the dish in the smoker and smoke for 3-4

hours, basting the drumsticks with the glaze every 30 minutes. Cook until the internal temperature reaches 165°F (74°C) and the turkey is cooked through and tender.

Smoked Moroccan Spiced Chicken Thighs

Ingredients:

8 chicken thighs, 1 tbsp ground cumin, 1 tbsp ground coriander, 1 tbsp smoked paprika, 1 tsp ground cinnamon, 1 tsp ground ginger, 1/2 tsp cayenne pepper, 1/2 tsp salt, 1/4 tsp black pepper, 2 tbsp olive oil, 2 tbsp lemon juice.

Directions:

Preheat the electric smoker to 275°F (135°C). In a small bowl, combine ground cumin, ground coriander, smoked paprika, ground cinnamon, ground ginger, cayenne pepper, salt, black pepper, olive oil, and lemon juice to make a marinade. Place the chicken thighs in a resealable bag and pour the marinade over them. Seal the bag and massage the marinade into the chicken thighs. Let them marinate in the refrigerator for 1-2 hours. Remove the chicken thighs from the marinade and discard the marinade. Place the chicken thighs in the smoker and smoke for 2-3 hours, or until the internal temperature reaches 165°F (74°C) and the chicken is cooked through and tender. Remove from the smoker and let them rest for a few minutes before serving.

Smoked Herb-Stuffed Cornish Game Hens

Ingredients:

4 Cornish game hens, 4 sprigs fresh rosemary, 4 sprigs fresh thyme, 4 sprigs fresh sage, 4 cloves garlic (minced), 2 tbsp olive oil, 1 tsp salt, 1/2 tsp black pepper.

Directions:

Preheat the electric smoker to 275°F (135°C). Rinse the Cornish game hens and pat them dry with paper towels. In a small bowl, combine minced garlic, olive oil, salt, and black pepper to make a herb mixture. Carefully loosen the skin from the breasts of the hens, being careful not to tear it. Insert sprigs of rosemary, thyme, and sage under the skin of each hen. Rub the herb mixture all over the hens, including inside the cavity. Place the hens in the smoker and smoke for 2-3 hours, or until the internal temperature reaches 165°F (74°C) and the skin is golden brown and crispy. Remove from the smoker and let them rest for a few minutes before serving.

Smoked Honey Garlic Chicken Wings

Ingredients:

2 lbs chicken wings, 1/4 cup honey, 2 tbsp soy sauce, 2 tbsp olive oil, 2 cloves garlic (minced), 1 tsp smoked paprika, 1/2 tsp salt, 1/4 tsp black pepper.

Directions:

Preheat the electric smoker to 275°F (135°C). In a bowl, whisk together honey, soy sauce, olive oil, minced garlic, smoked paprika, salt, and black pepper to make a marinade. Place the chicken wings in a resealable bag and pour the marinade over them. Seal the bag and massage the marinade into the wings. Let them marinate in the refrigerator for 1-2 hours. Remove the chicken wings from the marinade and discard the marinade. Place the wings in the smoker and smoke for 2-3 hours, or until the internal temperature reaches 165°F (74°C) and the wings are cooked through and crispy. Remove from the smoker and let them rest for a few minutes before serving.

Smoked Garlic and Herb Lamb Chops

Ingredients:

8 lamb chops, 4 cloves garlic (minced), 2 tbsp chopped fresh rosemary, 2 tbsp chopped fresh thyme, 2 tbsp olive oil, 1 tsp salt, 1/2 tsp black pepper.

Directions:

Preheat the electric smoker to 275°F (135°C). In a small bowl, combine minced garlic, chopped rosemary, chopped thyme, olive oil, salt, and black pepper to make a marinade. Rub the marinade all over the lamb chops, ensuring even coverage. Place the lamb chops in the smoker and smoke for 1-2 hours, or until the internal temperature reaches your desired level of doneness. For medium-rare, aim for an internal temperature of 145°F (63°C). Adjust the cooking time accordingly. Remove from the smoker and let them rest for a few minutes before serving.

Smoked Maple Dijon Glazed Turkey Breast

Ingredients:

1 bone-in turkey breast (about 6 lbs), 1/4 cup maple syrup, 2 tbsp Dijon mustard, 2 tbsp olive oil, 1 tbsp apple cider vinegar, 1 tsp dried thyme, 1/2 tsp garlic powder, 1/2 tsp onion powder, 1/2 tsp salt, 1/4 tsp black pepper.

Directions:

Preheat the electric smoker to 275°F (135°C). In a small bowl, whisk together maple syrup, Dijon mustard, olive oil, apple cider vinegar, dried thyme, garlic powder, onion powder, salt, and black pepper to make a glaze. Place the turkey breast in a baking dish and brush it with the glaze, reserving some for basting. Place the dish in the smoker and smoke for 4-5 hours, basting the turkey breast with the glaze every 30 minutes. Cook until the internal temperature reaches 165°F (74°C) in the thickest part of the breast. Remove from the smoker and let it rest for 20 minutes before slicing.

Smoked Spicy Paprika Chicken Drumsticks

Ingredients:

8 chicken drumsticks, 2 tbsp smoked paprika, 1 tbsp chili powder, 1 tbsp brown sugar, 1 tsp garlic powder, 1 tsp onion powder, 1 tsp salt, 1/2 tsp black pepper, 2 tbsp olive oil.

Directions:

Preheat the electric smoker to 275°F (135°C). In a small bowl, combine smoked paprika, chili powder, brown sugar, garlic powder, onion powder, salt, black pepper, and olive oil to make a spice rub. Rub the spice mixture all over the chicken drumsticks, ensuring even coverage. Place the drumsticks in the smoker and smoke for 2-3 hours, or until the internal temperature reaches 165°F (74°C) and the chicken is cooked through. Remove from the smoker and let them rest for a few minutes before serving.

Smoked Rosemary Lemon Chicken Thighs

Ingredients:

8 chicken thighs, 2 tbsp chopped fresh rosemary, 2 lemons (zested and juiced), 4 cloves garlic (minced), 2 tbsp olive oil, 1 tsp salt, 1/2 tsp black pepper.

Directions:

Preheat the electric smoker to 275°F (135°C). In a small bowl, combine chopped rosemary, lemon zest, lemon juice, minced garlic, olive oil, salt, and black pepper to make a marinade. Place the chicken thighs in a resealable bag and pour the marinade over them. Seal the bag and massage the marinade into the chicken thighs. Let them marinate in the refrigerator for 1-2 hours. Remove the chicken thighs from the marinade and discard the marinade. Place the chicken thighs in the smoker and smoke for 2-3 hours, or until the internal temperature reaches 165°F (74°C) and the chicken is cooked through. Remove from the smoker and let them rest for a few minutes before serving.

Smoked Greek-style Lemon Garlic Chicken

Ingredients:

4 bone-in, skin-on chicken breasts, 2 lemons (zested and juiced), 4 cloves garlic (minced), 2 tbsp olive oil, 2 tsps dried oregano, 1 tsp dried thyme, 1 tsp salt, 1/2 tsp black pepper.

Directions:

Preheat the electric smoker to 275°F (135°C). In a small bowl, combine lemon zest, lemon juice, minced garlic, olive oil, dried oregano, dried thyme, salt, and black pepper to make a marinade. Place the chicken breasts in a resealable bag and pour the marinade over them. Seal the bag and massage the marinade into the chicken breasts. Let them marinate in the refrigerator for 1-2 hours. Remove the chicken breasts from the marinade and discard the marinade. Place the chicken breasts in the smoker and smoke for 2-3 hours, or until the internal temperature reaches 165°F (74°C) and the chicken is cooked through. Remove from the smoker and let them rest for a few minutes before serving.

Smoked Moroccan Spiced Turkey Legs

Ingredients:

4 turkey legs, 1 tbsp ground cumin, 1 tbsp ground coriander, 1 tbsp smoked paprika, 1 tbsp ground cinnamon, 1 tbsp ground ginger, 1/2 tsp cayenne pepper, 1 tsp salt, 1/2 tsp black pepper, 2 tbsp olive oil.

Directions:

Preheat the electric smoker to 275°F (135°C). In a small bowl, combine ground cumin, ground coriander, smoked paprika, ground cinnamon, ground ginger, cayenne pepper, salt, black pepper, and olive oil to make a spice rub. Rub the spice mixture all over the turkey legs, ensuring even coverage. Place the turkey legs in the smoker and smoke for 3-4 hours, or until the internal temperature reaches 165°F (74°C) and the turkey is cooked through. Remove from the smoker and let them rest for a few minutes before serving.

Smoked Garlic Herb Turkey Burgers

Ingredients:

1.5 lbs ground turkey, 4 cloves garlic (minced), 2 tbsp chopped fresh parsley, 2 tbsp chopped fresh sage, 1 tsp dried thyme, 1 tsp salt, 1/2 tsp black pepper, 2 tbsp olive oil.

Directions:

Preheat the electric smoker to 275°F (135°C). In a large bowl, combine ground turkey, minced garlic, chopped fresh parsley, chopped fresh sage, dried thyme, salt, and black pepper. Mix well to incorporate all the ingredients. Form the mixture into burger patties of your desired size and thickness. Brush both sides of the patties with olive oil. Place the turkey burgers in the smoker and smoke for 1-2 hours, or until the internal temperature reaches 165°F (74°C) and the burgers are cooked through. Remove from the smoker and let them rest for a few minutes before serving.

Smoked Lemon Herb Cornish Game Hens

Ingredients:

4 Cornish game hens, 2 lemons (zested and juiced), 4 cloves garlic (minced), 2 tbsp chopped fresh thyme, 2 tbsp chopped fresh rosemary, 1 tsp salt, 1/2 tsp black pepper, 4 tbsp butter (melted).
Directions:
Preheat the electric smoker to 275°F (135°C). In a small bowl, combine lemon zest, lemon juice, minced garlic, chopped fresh thyme, chopped fresh rosemary, salt, black pepper, and melted butter to make a marinade. Rub the marinade all over the Cornish game hens, including under the skin. Place the hens in the smoker and smoke for 2-3 hours, or until the internal temperature reaches 165°F (74°C) and the skin is golden brown and crispy. Remove from the smoker and let them rest for a few minutes before serving.

Smoked Teriyaki Turkey Drumsticks

Ingredients:
4 turkey drumsticks, 1 cup soy sauce, 1/4 cup honey, 2 tbsp rice vinegar, 2 tbsp sesame oil, 2 cloves garlic (minced), 1 tsp grated fresh ginger, 1/2 tsp black pepper.
Directions:
Preheat the electric smoker to 275°F (135°C). In a bowl, whisk together soy sauce, honey, rice vinegar, sesame oil, minced garlic, grated ginger, and black pepper to make a teriyaki marinade. Place the turkey drumsticks in a resealable bag and pour the marinade over them. Seal the bag and massage the marinade into the drumsticks. Let them marinate in the refrigerator for 1-2 hours. Remove the drumsticks from the marinade and discard the marinade. Place the drumsticks in the smoker and smoke for 3-4 hours, or until the internal temperature reaches 165°F (74°C) and the turkey is cooked through. Remove from the smoker and let them rest for a few minutes before serving.

Smoked Herb-Rubbed Turkey Breast

Ingredients:
1 bone-in turkey breast (about 6 lbs), 2 tbsp olive oil, 2 tsps dried thyme, 2 tsps dried sage, 1 tsp dried rosemary, 1 tsp dried marjoram, 1 tsp salt, 1/2 tsp black pepper.
Directions:
Preheat the electric smoker to 275°F (135°C). In a small bowl, combine dried thyme, dried sage, dried rosemary, dried marjoram, salt, black pepper, and olive oil to make a herb rub. Rub the herb mixture all over the turkey breast, ensuring even coverage. Place the turkey breast in the smoker and smoke for 4-5 hours, or until the internal temperature reaches 165°F (74°C) in the thickest part of the breast. Remove from the smoker and let it rest for 20 minutes before slicing.

Smoked Cajun Chicken Drumsticks

Ingredients:
8 chicken drumsticks, 2 tbsp paprika, 1 tbsp garlic powder, 1 tbsp onion powder, 1 tbsp dried oregano, 1 tbsp dried thyme, 2 tsps cayenne pepper, 2 tsps salt, 1 tsp black pepper, 2 tbsp olive oil.
Directions:
Preheat the electric smoker to 275°F (135°C). In a small bowl, combine paprika, garlic powder, onion powder, dried oregano, dried thyme, cayenne pepper, salt, black pepper, and olive oil to make a Cajun spice rub. Rub the spice mixture all over the chicken drumsticks, ensuring even coverage. Place the drumsticks in the smoker and smoke for 2-3 hours, or until the internal temperature reaches 165°F (74°C) and the chicken is cooked through. Remove from the smoker and let them rest for a few minutes before serving.

Smoked Herb-Stuffed Turkey Legs

Ingredients:

4 turkey legs, 4 cloves garlic (minced), 2 tbsp chopped fresh parsley, 2 tbsp chopped fresh sage, 2 tbsp chopped fresh thyme, 2 tbsp chopped fresh rosemary, 2 tbsp olive oil, 1 tsp salt, 1/2 tsp black pepper.

Directions:

Preheat the electric smoker to 275°F (135°C). In a small bowl, combine minced garlic, chopped fresh parsley, chopped fresh sage, chopped fresh thyme, chopped fresh rosemary, olive oil, salt, and black pepper to make a herb mixture. Carefully loosen the skin from the turkey legs, being careful not to tear it. Spread the herb mixture evenly under the skin of each turkey leg. Place the turkey legs in the smoker and smoke for 3-4 hours, or until the internal temperature reaches 165°F (74°C) and the turkey is cooked through. Remove from the smoker and let them rest for a few minutes before serving.

Smoked Honey Mustard Turkey Breast

Ingredients:

1 bone-in turkey breast (about 6 lbs), 1/4 cup honey, 2 tbsp Dijon mustard, 2 tbsp olive oil, 1 tbsp apple cider vinegar, 1 tsp smoked paprika, 1/2 tsp garlic powder, 1/2 tsp onion powder, 1/2 tsp salt, 1/4 tsp black pepper.

Directions:

Preheat the electric smoker to 275°F (135°C). In a bowl, whisk together honey, Dijon mustard, olive oil, apple cider vinegar, smoked paprika, garlic powder, onion powder, salt, and black pepper to make a glaze. Place the turkey breast in a baking dish and brush it with the glaze, reserving some for basting. Place the dish in the smoker and smoke for 4-5 hours, basting the turkey breast with the glaze every 30 minutes. Cook until the internal temperature reaches 165°F (74°C) in the thickest part of the breast. Remove from the smoker and let it rest for 20 minutes before slicing.

Smoked Herb-Marinated Lamb Shoulder

Ingredients:

1 lamb shoulder (about 4 lbs), 4 cloves garlic (minced), 2 tbsp chopped fresh rosemary, 2 tbsp chopped fresh thyme, 2 tbsp chopped fresh parsley, 2 tbsp olive oil, 1 tsp salt, 1/2 tsp black pepper.

Directions:

Preheat the electric smoker to 275°F (135°C). In a small bowl, combine minced garlic, chopped rosemary, chopped thyme, chopped parsley, olive oil, salt, and black pepper to make a marinade. Rub the marinade all over the lamb shoulder, ensuring even coverage. Place the lamb shoulder in the smoker and smoke for 4-5 hours, or until the internal temperature reaches 165°F (74°C) and the lamb is tender. Remove from the smoker and let it rest for 20 minutes before carving.

Smoked Lemon Herb Chicken Skewers

Ingredients:

2 lbs boneless, skinless chicken breasts (cut into 1-inch cubes), 2 lemons (zested and juiced), 4 cloves garlic (minced), 2 tbsp chopped fresh rosemary, 2 tbsp chopped fresh thyme, 2 tbsp olive oil, 1 tsp salt, 1/2 tsp black pepper.

Directions:

Preheat the electric smoker to 275°F (135°C). In a small bowl, combine lemon zest, lemon juice, minced garlic, chopped rosemary, chopped thyme, olive oil, salt, and black pepper to make a marinade. Thread the chicken cubes onto skewers. Place the skewers in the smoker and smoke for 2-3 hours, or until the internal temperature reaches 165°F (74°C) and the chicken is cooked through. Remove from the smoker and let them rest for a few minutes before serving.

Smoked Greek-style Lamb Burgers

Ingredients:

1.5 lbs ground lamb, 1/2 cup crumbled feta cheese, 1/4 cup chopped Kalamata olives, 2 tbsp chopped fresh parsley, 2 tbsp chopped fresh mint, 2 cloves garlic (minced), 1 tsp dried oregano, 1/2 tsp salt, 1/4 tsp black pepper.

Directions:

Preheat the electric smoker to 275°F (135°C). In a large bowl, combine ground lamb, crumbled feta cheese, chopped Kalamata olives, chopped fresh parsley, chopped fresh mint, minced garlic, dried oregano, salt, and black pepper. Mix well to ensure all ingredients are evenly distributed. Form the mixture into burger patties of your desired size and thickness. Place the lamb burgers in the smoker and smoke for 1-2 hours, or until the internal temperature reaches 160°F (71°C) for medium doneness. Adjust the cooking time based on your preference. Remove from the smoker and let them rest for a few minutes before serving.

Smoked Garlic Herb Chicken Quarters

Ingredients:

4 chicken leg quarters, 4 cloves garlic (minced), 2 tbsp chopped fresh rosemary, 2 tbsp chopped fresh thyme, 2 tbsp olive oil, 1 tsp salt, 1/2 tsp black pepper.

Directions:

Preheat the electric smoker to 275°F (135°C). In a small bowl, combine minced garlic, chopped rosemary, chopped thyme, olive oil, salt, and black pepper to make a marinade. Rub the marinade all over the chicken leg quarters, ensuring even coverage. Place the leg quarters in the smoker and smoke for 2-3 hours, or until the internal temperature reaches 165°F (74°C) and the chicken is cooked through. Remove from the smoker and let them rest for a few minutes before serving.

Smoked Moroccan Lamb Stew

Ingredients:

2 lbs lamb stew meat, 2 onions (chopped), 4 cloves garlic (minced), 2 carrots (sliced), 2 potatoes (diced), 1 can diced tomatoes, 2 cups beef broth, 2 tbsp olive oil, 1 tbsp ground cumin, 1 tbsp ground coriander, 1 tsp ground cinnamon, 1 tsp paprika, 1/2 tsp turmeric, 1/2 tsp salt, 1/4 tsp black pepper, fresh cilantro (for garnish).

Directions:

Preheat the electric smoker to 275°F (135°C). In a large Dutch oven or oven-safe pot, heat olive oil over medium heat. Add the lamb stew meat and brown it on all sides. Remove the lamb from the pot and set it aside. In the same pot, add the onions and garlic. Sauté until the onions are translucent. Add the carrots, potatoes, diced tomatoes, beef broth, ground cumin, ground coriander, ground cinnamon, paprika, turmeric, salt, and black pepper. Stir well to combine. Return the lamb to the pot. Cover the pot and place it in the smoker. Smoke for 3-4 hours, or until the lamb is tender and the flavors have melded together. Serve the Moroccan lamb stew hot, garnished with fresh cilantro.

Smoked Lemon Garlic Shrimp Skewers

Ingredients:

1 lb large shrimp (peeled and deveined), 2 lemons (zested and juiced), 4 cloves garlic (minced), 2 tbsp chopped fresh parsley, 2 tbsp olive oil, 1 tsp salt, 1/2 tsp black pepper.

Directions:

Preheat the electric smoker to 275°F (135°C). In a small bowl, combine lemon zest, lemon juice, minced garlic, chopped fresh parsley, olive oil, salt, and black pepper to make a marinade. Thread the shrimp onto skewers. Place the skewers in the smoker and smoke for 20-30 minutes, or until the shrimp are opaque and cooked through. Remove from the smoker and let them rest for a few minutes before serving.

Smoked Herb-Rubbed Lamb Rack

Ingredients:

2 racks of lamb (about 1.5 lbs each), 2 tbsp chopped fresh rosemary, 2 tbsp chopped fresh thyme, 2 cloves garlic (minced), 2 tbsp olive oil, 1 tsp salt, 1/2 tsp black pepper.

Directions:

Preheat the electric smoker to 275°F (135°C). In a small bowl, combine chopped rosemary, chopped thyme, minced garlic, olive oil, salt, and black pepper to make a herb rub. Rub the herb mixture all over the lamb racks, ensuring even coverage. Place the lamb racks in the smoker and smoke for 2-3 hours, or until the internal temperature reaches your desired level of doneness. For medium-rare, aim for an internal temperature of 145°F (63°C). Adjust the cooking time accordingly. Remove from the smoker and let them rest for a few minutes before slicing.

Smoked Lemon Herb Butter Turkey

Ingredients:

1 whole turkey (12-14 lbs), 2 lemons (zested and juiced), 4 cloves garlic (minced), 4 tbsp butter (softened), 2 tbsp chopped fresh rosemary, 2 tbsp chopped fresh thyme, 2 tbsp chopped fresh parsley, 1 tsp salt, 1/2 tsp black pepper.

Directions:

Preheat the electric smoker to 275°F (135°C). In a small bowl, combine lemon zest, lemon juice, minced garlic, softened butter, chopped rosemary, chopped thyme, chopped parsley, salt, and black pepper to make a lemon herb butter mixture. Gently loosen the skin of the turkey, being careful not to tear it. Spread the lemon herb butter mixture evenly under the skin, covering as much of the turkey as possible. Place the turkey in the smoker and smoke for approximately 4-5 hours, or until the internal temperature reaches 165°F (74°C) in the thickest part of the thigh. Remove from the smoker and let it rest for 20-30 minutes before carving.

Smoked Honey Glazed Lamb Ribs

Ingredients:

2 racks of lamb ribs (about 3 lbs total), 1/4 cup honey, 2 tbsp soy sauce, 2 tbsp Dijon mustard, 2 cloves garlic (minced), 1 tsp smoked paprika, 1/2 tsp salt, 1/4 tsp black pepper.

Directions:

Preheat the electric smoker to 275°F (135°C). In a bowl, whisk together honey, soy sauce, Dijon mustard, minced garlic, smoked paprika, salt, and black pepper to make a glaze. Place the lamb ribs in a baking dish and brush them with the glaze, reserving some for basting. Place the dish in the smoker and smoke for 3-4 hours, basting the ribs with the glaze every 30 minutes. Cook until the meat is tender and pulls away from the bones. Remove from the smoker and let them rest for a few minutes before serving.

Smoked Herb-Marinated Chicken Tenders

Ingredients:

1 lb chicken tenders, 2 tbsp chopped fresh basil, 2 tbsp chopped fresh parsley, 2 tbsp chopped fresh oregano, 2 cloves garlic (minced), 2 tbsp olive oil, 1 tsp salt, 1/2 tsp black pepper.

Directions:

Preheat the electric smoker to 275°F (135°C). In a small bowl, combine chopped basil, chopped parsley, chopped oregano, minced garlic, olive oil, salt, and black pepper to make a marinade. Place the chicken tenders in a resealable bag and pour the marinade over them. Seal the bag and massage the marinade into the chicken tenders. Let them marinate in the refrigerator for 1-2 hours. Remove the chicken tenders from the marinade and discard the marinade. Place the chicken tenders in the smoker and smoke for 1-2 hours, or until the internal temperature reaches 165°F (74°C) and the chicken is cooked through. Remove from the smoker and let them rest for a few minutes before serving.

CHAPTER 6: TURKEY RECIPES

Smoked Maple-Bourbon Glazed Turkey Breast
Ingredients:

1 bone-in turkey breast (about 6 lbs), 1/2 cup maple syrup, 1/4 cup bourbon, 2 tbsp Dijon mustard, 2 tbsp soy sauce, 2 tbsp olive oil, 1 tbsp apple cider vinegar, 1 tsp smoked paprika, 1/2 tsp garlic powder, 1/2 tsp onion powder, 1/2 tsp salt, 1/4 tsp black pepper.

Directions:

Preheat the electric smoker to 275°F (135°C). In a bowl, whisk together maple syrup, bourbon, Dijon mustard, soy sauce, olive oil, apple cider vinegar, smoked paprika, garlic powder, onion powder, salt, and black pepper to make a glaze. Place the turkey breast in a baking dish and brush it with the glaze, reserving some for basting. Place the dish in the smoker and smoke for 4-5 hours, basting the turkey breast with the glaze every 30 minutes. Cook until the internal temperature reaches 165°F (74°C) in the thickest part of the breast. Remove from the smoker and let it rest for 20 minutes before slicing.

Smoked Herb-Roasted Turkey Legs
Ingredients:

4 turkey legs, 4 tbsp butter (softened), 2 tbsp chopped fresh thyme, 2 tbsp chopped fresh rosemary, 2 tbsp chopped fresh sage, 2 cloves garlic (minced), 1 tsp salt, 1/2 tsp black pepper.

Directions:

Preheat the electric smoker to 275°F (135°C). In a small bowl, combine softened butter, chopped thyme, chopped rosemary, chopped sage, minced garlic, salt, and black pepper to make an herb butter mixture. Gently loosen the skin from the turkey legs, being careful not to tear it. Spread the herb butter mixture evenly under the skin of each turkey leg. Place the turkey legs in the smoker and smoke for 3-4 hours, or until the internal temperature reaches 165°F (74°C) and the turkey is cooked through. Remove from the smoker and let them rest for a few minutes before serving.

Smoked Cajun Turkey Breast
Ingredients:

1 bone-in turkey breast (about 6 lbs), 2 tbsp paprika, 1 tbsp garlic powder, 1 tbsp onion powder, 1 tbsp dried oregano, 1 tbsp dried thyme, 2 tsps cayenne pepper, 2 tsps salt, 1 tsp black pepper, 2 tbsp olive oil.

Directions:

Preheat the electric smoker to 275°F (135°C). In a small bowl, combine paprika, garlic powder, onion powder, dried oregano, dried thyme, cayenne pepper, salt, black pepper, and olive oil to make a Cajun spice rub. Rub the spice mixture all over the turkey breast, ensuring even coverage. Place the turkey breast in the smoker and smoke for 4-5 hours, or until the internal temperature reaches 165°F (74°C) in the thickest part of the breast. Remove from the smoker and let it rest for 20 minutes before slicing.

Smoked Apple Cider Brined Whole Turkey
Ingredients:

1 whole turkey (12-14 lbs), 1 gallon apple cider, 1 cup kosher salt, 1/2 cup brown sugar, 4 bay leaves, 2 tbsp whole black peppercorns, 2 tbsp whole cloves, 2 tbsp whole allspice berries, 2 tbsp dried thyme, 2 tbsp dried rosemary, 2 tbsp dried sage, 2 tbsp olive oil, 1 tsp black pepper.

Directions:

In a large pot, combine apple cider, kosher salt, brown sugar, bay leaves, black peppercorns, cloves, allspice berries, dried thyme, dried rosemary, and dried sage. Bring the mixture to a boil, stirring until the salt and sugar are dissolved. Remove from heat and let the brine cool completely. Place the turkey in a brining bag or a large container and pour the brine over it, ensuring it is fully submerged. Seal the bag or cover the container and refrigerate for 12-24 hours.

Preheat the electric smoker to 275°F (135°C). Remove the turkey from the brine and pat it dry with paper towels. Rub the turkey with olive oil and sprinkle it with black pepper. Place the turkey in the smoker, breast side up, and smoke for approximately 4-5 hours, or until the internal temperature reaches 165°F (74°C) in the thickest part of the thigh. Rotate the turkey halfway through the cooking time for even smoking. Remove from the smoker and let it rest for 20-30 minutes before carving.

Smoked Herb-Stuffed Turkey Breast

Ingredients:

1 boneless turkey breast (about 4 lbs), 2 tbsp chopped fresh parsley, 2 tbsp chopped fresh sage, 2 tbsp chopped fresh thyme, 4 cloves garlic (minced), 1 tbsp olive oil, 1 tsp salt, 1/2 tsp black pepper.

Directions:

Preheat the electric smoker to 275°F (135°C). In a small bowl, combine chopped parsley, chopped sage, chopped thyme, minced garlic, olive oil, salt, and black pepper to make a herb stuffing. Butterfly the turkey breast by slicing it horizontally without cutting all the way through. Open the breast like a book and spread the herb stuffing evenly over the inside. Close the breast and secure it with kitchen twine. Place the turkey breast in the smoker and smoke for 3-4 hours, or until the internal temperature reaches 165°F (74°C) and the turkey is cooked through. Remove from the smoker and let it rest for 20 minutes before slicing.

Smoked Cranberry Glazed Turkey Wings

Ingredients:

2 lbs turkey wings, 1 cup cranberry sauce, 1/4 cup maple syrup, 2 tbsp soy sauce, 2 tbsp apple cider vinegar, 2 cloves garlic (minced), 1 tsp dried thyme, 1/2 tsp salt, 1/4 tsp black pepper.

Directions:

Preheat the electric smoker to 275°F (135°C). In a bowl, whisk together cranberry sauce, maple syrup, soy sauce, apple cider vinegar, minced garlic, dried thyme, salt, and black pepper to make a glaze. Place the turkey wings in a baking dish and brush them with the glaze, reserving some for basting. Place the dish in the smoker and smoke for 2-3 hours, basting the wings with the glaze every 30 minutes. Cook until the meat is tender and pulls away from the bones. Remove from the smoker and let them rest for a few minutes before serving.

Smoked Lemon Herb Turkey Drumsticks

Ingredients:

4 turkey drumsticks, 2 lemons (zested and juiced), 4 cloves garlic (minced), 2 tbsp chopped fresh rosemary, 2 tbsp chopped fresh thyme, 2 tbsp olive oil, 1 tsp salt, 1/2 tsp black pepper.

Directions:

Preheat the electric smoker to 275°F (135°C). In a small bowl, combine lemon zest, lemon juice, minced garlic, chopped fresh rosemary, chopped fresh thyme, olive oil, salt, and black pepper to make a marinade. Place the turkey drumsticks in a resealable bag and pour the marinade over them. Seal the bag and massage the marinade into the drumsticks. Let them marinate in the refrigerator for 1-2 hours. Remove the drumsticks from the marinade and discard the marinade. Place the drumsticks in the smoker and smoke for 3-4 hours, or until the internal temperature reaches 165°F (74°C) and the turkey is cooked through. Remove from the smoker and let them rest for a few minutes before serving.

Smoked Orange Glazed Turkey Breast
Ingredients:

1 bone-in turkey breast (about 6 lbs), 1 cup orange marmalade, 2 tbsp soy sauce, 2 tbsp Dijon mustard, 2 tbsp olive oil, 2 tbsp orange juice, 1 tsp smoked paprika, 1/2 tsp garlic powder, 1/2 tsp onion powder, 1/2 tsp salt, 1/4 tsp black pepper.

Directions:

Preheat the electric smoker to 275°F (135°C). In a bowl, whisk together orange marmalade, soy sauce, Dijon mustard, olive oil, orange juice, smoked paprika, garlic powder, onion powder, salt, and black pepper to make a glaze. Place the turkey breast in a baking dish and brush it with the glaze, reserving some for basting. Place the dish in the smoker and smoke for 4-5 hours, basting the turkey breast with the glaze every 30 minutes. Cook until the internal temperature reaches 165°F (74°C) in the thickest part of the breast. Remove from the smoker and let it rest for 20 minutes before slicing.

Smoked Herb-Rubbed Turkey Legs
Ingredients:

4 turkey legs, 2 tbsp chopped fresh rosemary, 2 tbsp chopped fresh thyme, 2 tbsp chopped fresh sage, 2 cloves garlic (minced), 2 tbsp olive oil, 1 tsp salt, 1/2 tsp black pepper.

Directions:

Preheat the electric smoker to 275°F (135°C). In a small bowl, combine chopped fresh rosemary, chopped fresh thyme, chopped fresh sage, minced garlic, olive oil, salt, and black pepper to make a herb rub. Rub the herb mixture all over the turkey legs, ensuring even coverage. Place the turkey legs in the smoker and smoke for 3-4 hours, or until the internal temperature reaches 165°F (74°C) and the turkey is cooked through. Remove from the smoker and let them rest for a few minutes before serving.

Smoked Teriyaki Turkey Wings
Ingredients:

2 lbs turkey wings, 1 cup soy sauce, 1/2 cup pineapple juice, 1/4 cup honey, 2 tbsp rice vinegar, 2 tbsp sesame oil, 2 cloves garlic (minced), 1 tsp grated fresh ginger, 1/2 tsp black pepper.

Directions:

Preheat the electric smoker to 275°F (135°C). In a bowl, whisk together soy sauce, pineapple juice, honey, rice vinegar, sesame oil, minced garlic, grated ginger, and black pepper to make a teriyaki marinade. Place the turkey wings in a resealable bag and pour the marinade over them. Seal the bag and massage the marinade into the wings. Let them marinate in the refrigerator for 1-2 hours. Remove the wings from the marinade and discard the marinade. Place the wings in the smoker and smoke for 2-3 hours, or until the internal temperature reaches 165°F (74°C) and the turkey is cooked through. Remove from the smoker and let them rest for a few minutes before serving.

Smoked Honey Mustard Turkey Breast
Ingredients:

1 bone-in turkey breast (about 6 lbs), 1/4 cup honey, 2 tbsp Dijon mustard, 2 tbsp olive oil, 2 tbsp apple cider vinegar, 1 tsp smoked paprika, 1/2 tsp garlic powder, 1/2 tsp onion powder, 1/2 tsp salt, 1/4 tsp black pepper.

Directions:

Preheat the electric smoker to 275°F (135°C). In a bowl, whisk together honey, Dijon mustard, olive oil, apple cider vinegar, smoked paprika, garlic powder, onion powder, salt, and black pepper to make a glaze. Place the turkey breast in a baking dish and brush it with the glaze, reserving some for basting. Place the dish in the smoker and smoke for 4-5 hours, basting the turkey breast with the glaze every 30 minutes. Cook until the internal temperature reaches 165°F (74°C) in the thickest part of the breast. Remove from the smoker and let it rest for 20 minutes before slicing.

Smoked Herb-Marinated Turkey Legs

Ingredients:

4 turkey legs, 4 cloves garlic (minced), 2 tbsp chopped fresh rosemary, 2 tbsp chopped fresh thyme, 2 tbsp chopped fresh parsley, 2 tbsp olive oil, 1 tsp salt, 1/2 tsp black pepper.

Directions:

Preheat the electric smoker to 275°F (135°C). In a small bowl, combine minced garlic, chopped fresh rosemary, chopped fresh thyme, chopped fresh parsley, olive oil, salt, and black pepper to make a marinade. Rub the marinade all over the turkey legs, ensuring even coverage. Place the turkey legs in the smoker and smoke for 3-4 hours, or until the internal temperature reaches 165°F (74°C) and the turkey is cooked through. Remove from the smoker and let them rest for a few minutes before serving.

Smoked Lemon Garlic Turkey Wings

Ingredients:

2 lbs turkey wings, 2 lemons (zested and juiced), 4 cloves garlic (minced), 2 tbsp chopped fresh thyme, 2 tbsp chopped fresh rosemary, 2 tbsp olive oil, 1 tsp salt, 1/2 tsp black pepper.

Directions:

Preheat the electric smoker to 275°F (135°C). In a small bowl, combine lemon zest, lemon juice, minced garlic, chopped fresh thyme, chopped fresh rosemary, olive oil, salt, and black pepper to make a marinade. Place the turkey wings in a resealable bag and pour the marinade over them. Seal the bag and massage the marinade into the wings. Let them marinate in the refrigerator for 1-2 hours. Remove the wings from the marinade and discard the marinade. Place the wings in the smoker and smoke for 2-3 hours, or until the internal temperature reaches 165°F (74°C) and the turkey is cooked through. Remove from the smoker and let them rest for a few minutes before serving.

Smoked Cranberry Glazed Turkey Breast

Ingredients:

1 boneless turkey breast (about 4 lbs), 1 cup cranberry juice, 1/2 cup cranberry sauce, 1/4 cup brown sugar, 2 tbsp Dijon mustard, 2 tbsp olive oil, 1 tsp dried thyme, 1/2 tsp salt, 1/4 tsp black pepper.

Directions:

Preheat the electric smoker to 275°F (135°C). In a small saucepan, combine cranberry juice, cranberry sauce, brown sugar, Dijon mustard, olive oil, dried thyme, salt, and black pepper. Cook over medium heat, stirring occasionally, until the mixture thickens and becomes a glaze. Place the turkey breast in the smoker and smoke for 2-3 hours, or until the internal temperature reaches 165°F (74°C) and the turkey is cooked through. Brush the cranberry glaze onto the turkey breast during the last hour of smoking, allowing it to caramelize. Remove from the smoker and let it rest for 20 minutes before slicing.

Smoked Herb-Rubbed Turkey Drumsticks
Ingredients:
4 turkey drumsticks, 2 tbsp chopped fresh thyme, 2 tbsp chopped fresh rosemary, 2 tbsp chopped fresh sage, 4 cloves garlic (minced), 2 tbsp olive oil, 1 tsp salt, 1/2 tsp black pepper.
Directions:
Preheat the electric smoker to 275°F (135°C). In a small bowl, combine chopped fresh thyme, chopped fresh rosemary, chopped fresh sage, minced garlic, olive oil, salt, and black pepper to make a herb rub. Rub the herb mixture all over the turkey drumsticks, ensuring even coverage. Place the drumsticks in the smoker and smoke for 3-4 hours, or until the internal temperature reaches 165°F (74°C) and the turkey is cooked through. Remove from the smoker and let them rest for a few minutes before serving.

Smoked Teriyaki Glazed Turkey Breast
Ingredients:
1 bone-in turkey breast (about 6 lbs), 1/2 cup soy sauce, 1/4 cup honey, 2 tbsp rice vinegar, 2 tbsp sesame oil, 2 tbsp minced fresh ginger, 4 cloves garlic (minced), 1 tsp black pepper.
Directions:
Preheat the electric smoker to 275°F (135°C). In a bowl, whisk together soy sauce, honey, rice vinegar, sesame oil, minced ginger, minced garlic, and black pepper to make a teriyaki marinade. Place the turkey breast in a resealable bag and pour the marinade over it. Seal the bag and massage the marinade into the turkey breast. Let it marinate in the refrigerator for 2-4 hours.
Remove the turkey breast from the marinade and discard the marinade. Place the turkey breast in the smoker and smoke for 4-5 hours, or until the internal temperature reaches 165°F (74°C) in the thickest part of the breast. Baste the turkey breast with any remaining marinade during the smoking process to enhance the flavor. Once done, remove from the smoker and let it rest for 20 minutes before slicing.

Smoked Herb Butter Turkey Legs
Ingredients:
4 turkey legs, 1/2 cup unsalted butter (softened), 2 tbsp chopped fresh thyme, 2 tbsp chopped fresh rosemary, 2 tbsp chopped fresh sage, 2 cloves garlic (minced), 1 tsp salt, 1/2 tsp black pepper.
Directions:
Preheat the electric smoker to 275°F (135°C). In a small bowl, combine softened butter, chopped fresh thyme, chopped fresh rosemary, chopped fresh sage, minced garlic, salt, and black pepper to make an herb butter mixture. Gently loosen the skin of the turkey legs, being careful not to tear it. Spread the herb butter mixture evenly under the skin of each turkey leg. Place the turkey legs in the smoker and smoke for 3-4 hours, or until the internal temperature reaches 165°F (74°C) and the turkey is cooked through. Remove from the smoker and let them rest for a few minutes before serving.

Smoked Maple Glazed Turkey Breast
Ingredients:
1 bone-in turkey breast (about 6 lbs), 1/2 cup maple syrup, 2 tbsp Dijon mustard, 2 tbsp apple cider vinegar, 2 tbsp olive oil, 1 tbsp smoked paprika, 1 tsp garlic powder, 1 tsp onion powder, 1/2 tsp salt, 1/4 tsp black pepper.

Directions:
Preheat the electric smoker to 275°F (135°C). In a bowl, whisk together maple syrup, Dijon mustard, apple cider vinegar, olive oil, smoked paprika, garlic powder, onion powder, salt, and black pepper to make a glaze. Place the turkey breast in a baking dish and brush it with the glaze, reserving some for basting. Place the dish in the smoker and smoke for 4-5 hours, basting the turkey breast with the glaze every 30 minutes. Cook until the internal temperature reaches 165°F (74°C) in the thickest part of the breast. Remove from the smoker and let it rest for 20 minutes before slicing.

Smoked Citrus-Herb Turkey Wings
Ingredients:
2 lbs turkey wings, 2 oranges (zested and juiced), 2 lemons (zested and juiced), 4 cloves garlic (minced), 2 tbsp chopped fresh thyme, 2 tbsp chopped fresh rosemary, 2 tbsp chopped fresh parsley, 2 tbsp olive oil, 1 tsp salt, 1/2 tsp black pepper.

Directions:
Preheat the electric smoker to 275°F (135°C). In a small bowl, combine the zest and juice of oranges and lemons, minced garlic, chopped fresh thyme, chopped fresh rosemary, chopped fresh parsley, olive oil, salt, and black pepper to make a marinade. Place the turkey wings in a resealable bag and pour the marinade over them. Seal the bag and massage the marinade into the wings. Let them marinate in the refrigerator for 2-4 hours.

Remove the wings from the marinade and discard the marinade. Place the wings in the smoker and smoke for 2-3 hours, or until the internal temperature reaches 165°F (74°C) and the turkey is cooked through. During the last 30 minutes of smoking, baste the wings with the remaining marinade to enhance the flavor and create a sticky glaze. Remove from the smoker and let them rest for a few minutes before serving.

Smoked Spicy Cranberry Turkey Drumsticks
Ingredients:
4 turkey drumsticks, 1 cup cranberry sauce, 2 tbsp hot sauce, 2 tbsp apple cider vinegar, 2 tbsp olive oil, 2 cloves garlic (minced), 1 tsp smoked paprika, 1/2 tsp cayenne pepper, 1/2 tsp salt, 1/4 tsp black pepper.

Directions:
Preheat the electric smoker to 275°F (135°C). In a bowl, whisk together cranberry sauce, hot sauce, apple cider vinegar, olive oil, minced garlic, smoked paprika, cayenne pepper, salt, and black pepper to make a spicy cranberry marinade. Place the turkey drumsticks in a resealable bag and pour the marinade over them. Seal the bag and massage the marinade into the drumsticks. Let them marinate in the refrigerator for 2-4 hours.

Remove the drumsticks from the marinade and discard the marinade. Place the drumsticks in the smoker and smoke for 3-4 hours, or until the internal temperature reaches 165°F (74°C) and the turkey is cooked through. During the last hour of smoking, brush the drumsticks with additional cranberry sauce mixed with hot sauce for added flavor and a beautiful glaze. Remove from the smoker and let them rest for a few minutes before serving.

Smoked Apple Butter Glazed Turkey Breast
Ingredients:

1 bone-in turkey breast (about 6 lbs), 1 cup apple butter, 2 tbsp Dijon mustard, 2 tbsp apple cider vinegar, 2 tbsp olive oil, 1 tbsp honey, 1 tsp smoked paprika, 1/2 tsp garlic powder, 1/2 tsp onion powder, 1/2 tsp salt, 1/4 tsp black pepper.

Directions:

Preheat the electric smoker to 275°F (135°C). In a bowl, whisk together apple butter, Dijon mustard, apple cider vinegar, olive oil, honey, smoked paprika, garlic powder, onion powder, salt, and black pepper to make a glaze. Place the turkey breast in a baking dish and brush it with the glaze, reserving some for basting. Place the dish in the smoker and smoke for 4-5 hours, basting the turkey breast with the glaze every 30 minutes. Cook until the internal temperature reaches 165°F (74°C) in the thickest part of the breast. Remove from the smoker and let it rest for 20 minutes before slicing.

Smoked Herb-Crusted Turkey Thighs

Ingredients:

4 turkey thighs, 2 tbsp chopped fresh thyme, 2 tbsp chopped fresh rosemary, 2 tbsp chopped fresh parsley, 2 cloves garlic (minced), 2 tbsp olive oil, 1 tsp salt, 1/2 tsp black pepper.

Directions:

Preheat the electric smoker to 275°F (135°C). In a small bowl, combine chopped fresh thyme, chopped fresh rosemary, chopped fresh parsley, minced garlic, olive oil, salt, and black pepper to make an herb crust. Rub the herb mixture all over the turkey thighs, ensuring even coverage. Place the turkey thighs in the smoker and smoke for 3-4 hours, or until the internal temperature reaches 165°F (74°C) and the turkey is cooked through. Remove from the smoker and let them rest for a few minutes before serving.

Smoked Honey Sriracha Turkey Wings

Ingredients:

2 lbs turkey wings, 1/4 cup honey, 2 tbsp Sriracha sauce, 2 tbsp soy sauce, 2 tbsp lime juice, 2 cloves garlic (minced), 1 tsp smoked paprika, 1/2 tsp salt, 1/4 tsp black pepper.

Directions:

Preheat the electric smoker to 275°F (135°C). In a bowl, whisk together honey, Sriracha sauce, soy sauce, lime juice, minced garlic, smoked paprika, salt, and black pepper to make a glaze. Place the turkey wings in a baking dish and brush them with the glaze, reserving some for basting. Place the dish in the smoker and smoke for 2-3 hours, basting the wings with the glaze every 30 minutes. Cook until the meat is tender and pulls away from the bones. Remove from the smoker and let them rest for a few minutes before serving.

Smoked Moroccan-Spiced Turkey Breast

Ingredients:

1 bone-in turkey breast (about 6 lbs), 2 tbsp ground cumin, 2 tbsp ground coriander, 2 tbsp ground paprika, 1 tbsp ground cinnamon, 1 tbsp ground ginger, 2 tsps ground turmeric, 1 tsp salt, 1/2 tsp black pepper, 2 tbsp olive oil.

Directions:

Preheat the electric smoker to 275°F (135°C). In a small bowl, combine ground cumin, ground coriander, ground paprika, ground cinnamon, ground ginger, ground turmeric, salt, black pepper, and olive oil to make a Moroccan spice rub. Rub the spice mixture all over the turkey breast, ensuring even coverage. Place the turkey breast in the smoker and smoke for 4-5 hours, or until the internal temperature reaches 165°F (74°C) in the thickest part of the breast. Remove from the smoker and let it rest for 20 minutes before slicing.

Smoked Pineapple-Glazed Turkey Wings
Ingredients:
2 lbs turkey wings, 1 cup pineapple juice, 1/4 cup brown sugar, 2 tbsp soy sauce, 2 tbsp ketchup, 2 tbsp apple cider vinegar, 2 cloves garlic (minced), 1 tsp smoked paprika, 1/2 tsp salt, 1/4 tsp black pepper.
Directions:
Preheat the electric smoker to 275°F (135°C). In a small saucepan, combine pineapple juice, brown sugar, soy sauce, ketchup, apple cider vinegar, minced garlic, smoked paprika, salt, and black pepper. Cook over medium heat, stirring occasionally, until the mixture thickens and becomes a glaze. Place the turkey wings in a baking dish and brush them with the glaze, reserving some for basting. Place the dish in the smoker and smoke for 2-3 hours, basting the wings with the glaze every 30 minutes. Cook until the meat is tender and pulls away from the bones. Remove from the smoker and let them rest for a few minutes before serving.

Smoked Herb-Stuffed Turkey Thighs
Ingredients:
4 turkey thighs, 2 tbsp chopped fresh parsley, 2 tbsp chopped fresh sage, 2 tbsp chopped fresh thyme, 4 cloves garlic (minced), 1 tbsp olive oil, 1 tsp salt, 1/2 tsp black pepper.
Directions:
Preheat the electric smoker to 275°F (135°C). In a small bowl, combine chopped parsley, chopped sage, chopped thyme, minced garlic, olive oil, salt, and black pepper to make an herb stuffing. Gently loosen the skin from the turkey thighs, being careful not to tear it. Spread the herb stuffing evenly under the skin of each turkey thigh. Place the thighs in the smoker and smoke for 3-4 hours, or until the internal temperature reaches 165°F (74°C) and the turkey is cooked through. Remove from the smoker and let them rest for a few minutes before serving.

Smoked Maple Mustard Turkey Drumsticks
Ingredients:
4 turkey drumsticks, 1/4 cup maple syrup, 2 tbsp Dijon mustard, 2 tbsp apple cider vinegar, 2 tbsp olive oil, 1 tsp smoked paprika, 1/2 tsp garlic powder, 1/2 tsp onion powder, 1/2 tsp salt, 1/4 tsp black pepper.
Directions:
Preheat the electric smoker to 275°F (135°C). In a bowl, whisk together maple syrup, Dijon mustard, apple cider vinegar, olive oil, smoked paprika, garlic powder, onion powder, salt, and black pepper to make a glaze. Place the turkey drumsticks in a baking dish and brush them with the glaze, reserving some for basting. Place the dish in the smoker and smoke for 3-4 hours, basting the drumsticks with the glaze every 30 minutes. Cook until the meat is tender and the internal temperature reaches 165°F (74°C). Remove from the smoker and let them rest for a few minutes before serving.

Smoked Herb-Marinated Turkey Breast
Ingredients:
1 boneless turkey breast (about 4 lbs), 2 tbsp chopped fresh rosemary, 2 tbsp chopped fresh thyme, 2 tbsp chopped fresh parsley, 4 cloves garlic (minced), 2 tbsp olive oil, 1 tsp salt, 1/2 tsp black pepper.
Directions:

Preheat the electric smoker to 275°F (135°C). In a small bowl, combine chopped rosemary, chopped thyme, chopped parsley, minced garlic, olive oil, salt, and black pepper to make an herb marinade. Place the turkey breast in a resealable bag and pour the marinade over it. Seal the bag and massage the marinade into the turkey breast. Let it marinate in the refrigerator for 2-4 hours.

Remove the turkey breast from the marinade and discard the marinade. Place the turkey breast in the smoker and smoke for 3-4 hours, or until the internal temperature reaches 165°F (74°C) in the thickest part of the breast. Remove from the smoker and let it rest for 20 minutes before slicing.

Smoked Honey Lime Turkey Wings

Ingredients: 2 lbs turkey wings, 1/4 cup honey, 2 tbsp lime juice, 2 tbsp soy sauce, 2 tbsp olive oil, 2 cloves garlic (minced), 1 tsp smoked paprika, 1/2 tsp salt, 1/4 tsp black pepper.

Directions:

Preheat the electric smoker to 275°F (135°C). In a bowl, whisk together honey, lime juice, soy sauce, olive oil, minced garlic, smoked paprika, salt, and black pepper to make a marinade. Place the turkey wings in a resealable bag and pour the marinade over them. Seal the bag and massage the marinade into the wings. Let them marinate in the refrigerator for 2-4 hours.

Remove the wings from the marinade and discard the marinade. Place the wings in the smoker and smoke for 2-3 hours, or until the internal temperature reaches 165°F (74°C) and the turkey is cooked through. Baste the wings with additional honey and lime juice mixture during the last 30 minutes of smoking. Remove from the smoker and let them rest for a few minutes before serving.

Smoked Cajun Turkey Breast

Ingredients:

1 bone-in turkey breast (about 6 lbs), 2 tbsp paprika, 1 tbsp garlic powder, 1 tbsp onion powder, 1 tbsp dried oregano, 1 tbsp dried thyme, 1 tbsp dried basil, 1 tbsp cayenne pepper, 1 tbsp black pepper, 1 tbsp salt, 2 tbsp olive oil.

Directions:

Preheat the electric smoker to 275°F (135°C). In a small bowl, combine paprika, garlic powder, onion powder, dried oregano, dried thyme, dried basil, cayenne pepper, black pepper, salt, and olive oil to make a Cajun spice rub. Rub the spice mixture all over the turkey breast, ensuring even coverage. Place the turkey breast in the smoker and smoke for 4-5 hours, or until the internal temperature reaches 165°F (74°C) in the thickest part of the breast. Remove from the smoker and let it rest for 20 minutes before slicing.

Smoked Chipotle-Orange Turkey Drumsticks

Ingredients:

4 turkey drumsticks, 2 chipotle peppers in adobo sauce (minced), 2 tbsp orange juice, 2 tbsp lime juice, 2 tbsp olive oil, 2 cloves garlic (minced), 1 tsp ground cumin, 1 tsp smoked paprika, 1/2 tsp salt, 1/4 tsp black pepper.

Directions:

Preheat the electric smoker to 275°F (135°C). In a small bowl, combine minced chipotle peppers, orange juice, lime juice, olive oil, minced garlic, ground cumin, smoked paprika, salt, and black pepper to make a marinade. Place the turkey drumsticks in a resealable bag and pour the marinade over them. Seal the bag and massage the marinade into the drumsticks. Let them marinate in the refrigerator for 2-4 hours.

Remove the drumsticks from the marinade and discard the marinade. Place the drumsticks in the smoker and smoke for 3-4 hours, or until the internal temperature reaches 165°F (74°C) and the turkey is cooked through. Remove from the smoker and let them rest for a few minutes before serving.

Smoked Balsamic-Glazed Turkey Breast
Ingredients:
1 bone-in turkey breast (about 6 lbs), 1/2 cup balsamic vinegar, 1/4 cup honey, 2 tbsp Dijon mustard, 2 tbsp olive oil, 2 cloves garlic (minced), 1 tsp dried thyme, 1/2 tsp salt, 1/4 tsp black pepper.
Directions:
Preheat the electric smoker to 275°F (135°C). In a small saucepan, combine balsamic vinegar, honey, Dijon mustard, olive oil, minced garlic, dried thyme, salt, and black pepper. Cook over medium heat, stirring occasionally, until the mixture thickens and becomes a glaze. Place the turkey breast in a baking dish and brush it with the glaze, reserving some for basting. Place the dish in the smoker and smoke for 4-5 hours, basting the turkey breast with the glaze every 30 minutes. Cook until the internal temperature reaches 165°F (74°C) in the thickest part of the breast. Remove from the smoker and let it rest for 20 minutes before slicing.

Smoked Lemon Pepper Turkey Wings
Ingredients:
2 lbs turkey wings, 2 lemons (zested and juiced), 2 tbsp black peppercorns (crushed), 2 tbsp olive oil, 2 cloves garlic (minced), 1 tsp salt.
Directions:
Preheat the electric smoker to 275°F (135°C). In a small bowl, combine lemon zest, lemon juice, crushed black peppercorns, olive oil, minced garlic, and salt to make a marinade. Place the turkey wings in a resealable bag and pour the marinade over them. Seal the bag and massage the marinade into the wings. Let them marinate in the refrigerator for 2-4 hours.
Remove the wings from the marinade and discard the marinade. Place the wings in the smoker and smoke for 2-3 hours, or until the internal temperature reaches 165°F (74°C) and the turkey is cooked through. The crushed black peppercorns will create a delicious crust on the wings as they smoke. Remove from the smoker and let them rest for a few minutes before serving.

Smoked Cranberry-Orange Glazed Turkey Breast
Ingredients:
1 bone-in turkey breast (about 6 lbs), 1 cup cranberry juice, 1/2 cup orange juice, 1/4 cup brown sugar, 2 tbsp Dijon mustard, 2 tbsp olive oil, 2 cloves garlic (minced), 1 tsp dried thyme, 1/2 tsp salt, 1/4 tsp black pepper.
Directions:
Preheat the electric smoker to 275°F (135°C). In a small saucepan, combine cranberry juice, orange juice, brown sugar, Dijon mustard, olive oil, minced garlic, dried thyme, salt, and black pepper. Cook over medium heat, stirring occasionally, until the mixture thickens and becomes a glaze. Place the turkey breast in a baking dish and brush it with the glaze, reserving some for basting. Place the dish in the smoker and smoke for 4-5 hours, basting the turkey breast with the glaze every 30 minutes. Cook until the internal temperature reaches 165°F (74°C) in the thickest part of the breast. Remove from the smoker and let it rest for 20 minutes before slicing.

Smoked Maple-Bourbon Turkey Legs

Ingredients:

4 turkey legs, 1/4 cup maple syrup, 2 tbsp bourbon, 2 tbsp soy sauce, 2 tbsp olive oil, 2 cloves garlic (minced), 1 tsp smoked paprika, 1/2 tsp salt, 1/4 tsp black pepper.

Directions:

Preheat the electric smoker to 275°F (135°C). In a bowl, whisk together maple syrup, bourbon, soy sauce, olive oil, minced garlic, smoked paprika, salt, and black pepper to make a marinade. Place the turkey legs in a resealable bag and pour the marinade over them. Seal the bag and massage the marinade into the legs. Let them marinate in the refrigerator for 2-4 hours.

Remove the legs from the marinade and discard the marinade. Place the legs in the smoker and smoke for 3-4 hours, or until the internal temperature reaches 165°F (74°C) and the turkey is cooked through. The combination of maple syrup and bourbon will create a rich and flavorful glaze on the legs as they smoke. Remove from the smoker and let them rest for a few minutes before serving.

Smoked Garlic-Herb Butter Turkey Breast

Ingredients:

1 bone-in turkey breast (about 6 lbs), 1/2 cup unsalted butter (softened), 4 cloves garlic (minced), 2 tbsp chopped fresh rosemary, 2 tbsp chopped fresh thyme, 1 tbsp chopped fresh sage, 1 tsp salt, 1/2 tsp black pepper.

Directions:

Preheat the electric smoker to 275°F (135°C). In a small bowl, combine softened butter, minced garlic, chopped rosemary, chopped thyme, chopped sage, salt, and black pepper to make a garlic-herb butter. Gently loosen the skin of the turkey breast, being careful not to tear it. Spread the garlic-herb butter evenly under the skin of the breast. Place the turkey breast in the smoker and smoke for 4-5 hours, or until the internal temperature reaches 165°F (74°C) in the thickest part of the breast. Remove from the smoker and let it rest for 20 minutes before slicing.

Smoked Maple-Dijon Glazed Turkey Wings

Ingredients:

2 lbs turkey wings, 1/4 cup maple syrup, 2 tbsp Dijon mustard, 2 tbsp apple cider vinegar, 2 tbsp olive oil, 2 cloves garlic (minced), 1 tsp smoked paprika, 1/2 tsp salt, 1/4 tsp black pepper.

Directions:

Preheat the electric smoker to 275°F (135°C). In a bowl, whisk together maple syrup, Dijon mustard, apple cider vinegar, olive oil, minced garlic, smoked paprika, salt, and black pepper to make a glaze. Place the turkey wings in a baking dish and brush them with the glaze, reserving some for basting. Place the dish in the smoker and smoke for 2-3 hours, basting the wings with the glaze every 30 minutes. Cook until the meat is tender and pulls away from the bones. Remove from the smoker and let them rest for a few minutes before serving.

Smoked Herb-Marinated Turkey Legs

Ingredients:

4 turkey legs, 2 tbsp chopped fresh parsley, 2 tbsp chopped fresh thyme, 2 tbsp chopped fresh rosemary, 4 cloves garlic (minced), 2 tbsp olive oil, 1 tsp salt, 1/2 tsp black pepper.

Directions:

Preheat the electric smoker to 275°F (135°C). In a small bowl, combine chopped parsley, chopped thyme, chopped rosemary, minced garlic, olive oil, salt, and black pepper to make an herb marinade. Place the turkey legs in a resealable bag and pour the marinade over them. Seal the bag and massage the marinade into the legs. Let them marinate in the refrigerator for 2-4 hours.

Remove the legs from the marinade and discard the marinade. Place the legs in the smoker and smoke for 3-4 hours, or until the internal temperature reaches 165°F (74°C) and the turkey is cooked through. The herb marinade will infuse the turkey legs with delicious flavor as they smoke. Remove from the smoker and let them rest for a few minutes before serving.

Smoked Honey Mustard Turkey Breast

Ingredients:

1 bone-in turkey breast (about 6 lbs), 1/4 cup honey, 2 tbsp Dijon mustard, 2 tbsp whole grain mustard, 2 tbsp apple cider vinegar, 2 tbsp olive oil, 2 cloves garlic (minced), 1 tsp smoked paprika, 1/2 tsp salt, 1/4 tsp black pepper.

Directions:

Preheat the electric smoker to 275°F (135°C). In a bowl, whisk together honey, Dijon mustard, whole grain mustard, apple cider vinegar, olive oil, minced garlic, smoked paprika, salt, and black pepper to make a honey mustard marinade. Place the turkey breast in a resealable bag and pour the marinade over it. Seal the bag and massage the marinade into the turkey breast. Let it marinate in the refrigerator for 2-4 hours.

Remove the turkey breast from the marinade and discard the marinade. Place the turkey breast in the smoker and smoke for 4-5 hours, or until the internal temperature reaches 165°F (74°C) in the thickest part of the breast. Remove from the smoker and let it rest for 20 minutes before slicing.

Smoked Orange-Ginger Glazed Turkey Drumsticks

Ingredients:

4 turkey drumsticks, 1/2 cup orange marmalade, 2 tbsp soy sauce, 2 tbsp rice vinegar, 2 tbsp olive oil, 2 tbsp grated fresh ginger, 2 cloves garlic (minced), 1 tsp orange zest, 1/2 tsp salt, 1/4 tsp black pepper.

Directions:

Preheat the electric smoker to 275°F (135°C). In a bowl, whisk together orange marmalade, soy sauce, rice vinegar, olive oil, grated ginger, minced garlic, orange zest, salt, and black pepper to make a glaze. Place the turkey drumsticks in a baking dish and brush them with the glaze, reserving some for basting. Place the dish in the smoker and smoke for 3-4 hours, basting the drumsticks with the glaze every 30 minutes. Cook until the meat is tender and pulls away from the bones. Remove from the smoker and let them rest for a few minutes before serving.

CHAPTER 7: FISH AND SEAFOOD RECIPES

Smoky Citrus Halibut

Ingredients:

4 halibut fillets, 2 tbsp olive oil, 2 tsps smoked paprika, 1 tsp garlic powder, zest of 1 lemon, zest of 1 orange, salt, black pepper.

Directions:

Preheat the electric smoker to 225°F. Rub the halibut fillets with olive oil. In a small bowl, combine smoked paprika, garlic powder, lemon zest, orange zest, salt, and black pepper. Sprinkle the spice mixture evenly over the halibut fillets. Place the fillets on the smoker racks and smoke for 1 hour or until the fish flakes easily with a fork.

Spicy Chipotle Grilled Shrimp

Ingredients:

1 lb large shrimp, 2 tbsp olive oil, 2 chipotle peppers in adobo sauce (minced), 2 cloves garlic (minced), 1 tsp smoked paprika, 1/2 tsp cayenne pepper, juice of 1 lime, salt.

Directions:

Preheat the electric smoker to 250°F. In a bowl, combine olive oil, minced chipotle peppers, minced garlic, smoked paprika, cayenne pepper, lime juice, and salt. Toss the shrimp in the marinade until well coated. Skewer the shrimp or place them in a smoker tray. Smoke for 20-25 minutes or until the shrimp are pink and cooked through.

Smoked Sesame Ginger Salmon

Ingredients:

4 salmon fillets, 2 tbsp soy sauce, 1 tbsp sesame oil, 1 tbsp fresh ginger (grated), 2 cloves garlic (minced), 1 tbsp honey, 1 tbsp sesame seeds, salt, black pepper.

Directions:

Preheat the electric smoker to 225°F. In a small bowl, whisk together soy sauce, sesame oil, grated ginger, minced garlic, honey, sesame seeds, salt, and black pepper. Place the salmon fillets on the smoker racks and brush the marinade over them. Smoke for 1 hour or until the salmon is cooked to your desired level of doneness.

Citrus Herb Smoked Swordfish

Ingredients:

4 swordfish steaks, juice of 2 oranges, juice of 1 lemon, juice of 1 lime, 2 tbsp olive oil, 2 tbsp fresh parsley (chopped), 1 tbsp fresh thyme (chopped), 1 tsp lemon zest, salt, black pepper.

Directions:

Preheat the electric smoker to 275°F. In a shallow dish, combine orange juice, lemon juice, lime juice, olive oil, chopped parsley, chopped thyme, lemon zest, salt, and black pepper. Add the swordfish steaks to the marinade and let them sit for 30 minutes. Place the steaks on the smoker racks and smoke for 20-25 minutes or until the fish is opaque and flakes easily.

Honey Lime Smoked Shrimp

Ingredients:

1 lb large shrimp, 3 tbsp honey, juice of 2 limes, 1 tbsp olive oil, 1 tsp smoked paprika, 1/2 tsp chili powder, 1/4 tsp cumin, salt, black pepper.

Directions:

Preheat the electric smoker to 250°F. In a bowl, whisk together honey, lime juice, olive oil, smoked paprika, chili powder, cumin, salt, and black pepper. Add the shrimp to the bowl and toss to coat. Skewer the shrimp or place them in a smoker tray. Smoke for 20-25 minutes or until the shrimp are

Herb-Infused Smoked Rainbow Trout

Ingredients:

4 rainbow trout fillets, 2 tbsp fresh dill (chopped), 2 tbsp fresh parsley (chopped), 1 tbsp fresh thyme leaves, 2 cloves garlic (minced), 2 tbsp lemon juice, 2 tbsp olive oil, salt, black pepper.

Directions:

Preheat the electric smoker to 225°F. In a small bowl, combine chopped dill, parsley, thyme, minced garlic, lemon juice, olive oil, salt, and black pepper. Rub the herb mixture onto the rainbow trout fillets, ensuring they are evenly coated. Place the fillets on the smoker racks and smoke for 1 hour or until the fish flakes easily with a fork.

Smoked Coconut Lime Shrimp

Ingredients:

1 lb large shrimp, 1 cup coconut milk, 2 tbsp lime juice, 1 tbsp soy sauce, 1 tbsp brown sugar, 2 tsps curry powder, 1 tsp garlic powder, 1/2 tsp turmeric, salt.

Directions:

Preheat the electric smoker to 250°F. In a bowl, whisk together coconut milk, lime juice, soy sauce, brown sugar, curry powder, garlic powder, turmeric, and salt. Add the shrimp to the bowl and marinate for 30 minutes. Skewer the shrimp or place them in a smoker tray. Smoke for 20-25 minutes or until the shrimp are pink and cooked through.

Smoked Maple Glazed Cedar Plank Salmon

Ingredients:

4 salmon fillets, 1 cedar plank (soaked in water for 1 hour), 1/4 cup maple syrup, 2 tbsp Dijon mustard, 2 tbsp soy sauce, 1 tbsp apple cider vinegar, 1 tsp garlic powder, salt, black pepper.

Directions:

Preheat the electric smoker to 225°F. In a small bowl, whisk together maple syrup, Dijon mustard, soy sauce, apple cider vinegar, garlic powder, salt, and black pepper. Place the soaked cedar plank on the smoker racks and lay the salmon fillets on top. Brush the maple glaze onto the salmon. Smoke for 1 hour or until the salmon is cooked through and flakes easily.

Jerk Spiced Smoked Red Snapper

Ingredients:

4 red snapper fillets, 2 tbsp jerk seasoning, 1 tbsp olive oil, juice of 1 lime, 1 tsp brown sugar, 1/2 tsp ground allspice, 1/2 tsp dried thyme, 1/4 tsp cayenne pepper, salt.

Directions:

Preheat the electric smoker to 250°F. In a bowl, combine jerk seasoning, olive oil, lime juice, brown sugar, allspice, dried thyme, cayenne pepper, and salt. Rub the jerk spice mixture onto the red snapper fillets. Place the fillets on the smoker racks and smoke for 30-35 minutes or until the fish is firm and opaque.

Smoked Cajun Crawfish Boil

Ingredients:

2 lbs crawfish, 4 corn cobs (halved), 4 red potatoes (quartered), 1 lb smoked sausage (sliced), 1 onion (quartered), 4 cloves garlic (minced), 2 tbsp Cajun seasoning, 2 tsps paprika, 1 tsp dried thyme, 1 tsp dried oregano, 1 tsp cayenne pepper, salt.

Directions:

Preheat the electric smoker to 250°F. In a large bowl, combine crawfish, corn cobs, red potatoes, smoked sausage, onion, minced garlic, Cajun seasoning, pap rika, dried thyme, dried oregano, cayenne pepper, and salt. Toss everything together to evenly coat with the seasonings. Transfer the mixture to a smoker tray or a large foil packet. Place the tray or packet on the smoker racks and smoke for 1-2 hours or until the crawfish are cooked through and the vegetables are tender.

Smoked Garlic Butter Scallops

Ingredients:

1 lb sea scallops, 4 tbsp butter, 4 cloves garlic (minced), 2 tbsp lemon juice, 1 tbsp chopped fresh parsley, salt, black pepper.

Directions:

Preheat the electric smoker to 225°F. In a small saucepan, melt the butter over low heat. Add minced garlic, lemon juice, chopped parsley, salt, and black pepper to the melted butter, stirring well. Place the scallops on the smoker racks and brush them generously with the garlic butter mixture. Smoke for 30-35 minutes or until the scallops are opaque and tender.

Asian-inspired Smoked Tuna Poke Bowl

Ingredients:

2 tuna steaks, 1/4 cup soy sauce, 2 tbsp rice vinegar, 1 tbsp sesame oil, 1 tbsp honey, 1 tsp grated ginger, 2 green onions (sliced), 1 avocado (sliced), 1 cup cooked sushi rice, 1 tbsp sesame seeds.

Directions:

Preheat the electric smoker to 275°F. In a bowl, whisk together soy sauce, rice vinegar, sesame oil, honey, grated ginger, and sliced green onions to create the marinade. Place the tuna steaks in the marinade and let them sit for 15-20 minutes. Remove the tuna from the marinade and place them on the smoker racks. Smoke for 15-20 minutes or until the tuna is cooked to your liking. Slice the smoked tuna and assemble the poke bowl with sushi rice, avocado slices, and sesame seeds. Drizzle with the remaining marinade.

Smoked Brown Sugar Glazed Swordfish

Ingredients:

4 swordfish steaks, 1/4 cup brown sugar, 2 tbsp Dijon mustard, 2 tbsp soy sauce, 1 tbsp olive oil, 1 tbsp lemon juice, 1 tsp garlic powder, salt, black pepper.

Directions:

Preheat the electric smoker to 225°F. In a small bowl, whisk together brown sugar, Dijon mustard, soy sauce, olive oil, lemon juice, garlic powder, salt, and black pepper to create the glaze. Place the swordfish steaks on the smoker racks and brush them generously with the glaze. Smoke for 1 hour or until the swordfish is cooked through and easily flakes with a fork.

Citrus Herb Smoked Mackerel

Ingredients:

4 mackerel fillets, zest of 1 lemon, zest of 1 orange, 2 tbsp fresh dill (chopped), 2 tbsp fresh parsley (chopped), 1 tbsp olive oil, salt, black pepper.

Directions:

Preheat the electric smoker to 225°F. In a small bowl, combine lemon zest, orange zest, chopped dill, chopped parsley, olive oil, salt, and black pepper. Rub the mixture onto the mackerel fillets, ensuring they are evenly coated. Place the fillets on the smoker racks and smoke for 1 hour or until the fish is cooked through and flakes easily.

Chili Lime Smoked Shrimp Tacos

Ingredients:

1 lb large shrimp, 2 tbsp chili powder, 1 tbsp lime zest, 2 tbsp lime juice, 1 tbsp olive oil, 1 tsp cumin, 1/2 tsp paprika, 1/2 tsp garlic powder, 1/2 tsp salt, 1/4 tsp cayenne pepper, 8 small flour tortillas, 1 cup shredded lettuce, 1/2 cup diced tomatoes, 1/4 cup chopped fresh cilantro, lime wedges for serving.

Directions:

Preheat the electric smoker to 250°F. In a bowl, combine chili powder, lime zest, lime juice, olive oil, cumin, paprika, garlic powder, salt, and cayenne pepper to make a marinade. Add the shrimp to the bowl and toss to coat evenly. Skewer the shrimp or place them in a smoker tray. Smoke for 20-25 minutes or until the shrimp are pink and cooked through. Warm the flour tortillas. Fill each tortilla with smoked shrimp, shredded lettuce, diced tomatoes, and chopped cilantro. Serve with lime wedges for squeezing over the tacos.

Smoked Honey Lime Salmon Skewers

Ingredients:

1 lb salmon fillets, cut into cubes, 1/4 cup honey, 2 tbsp lime juice, 1 tbsp soy sauce, 1 tbsp olive oil, 1 tsp grated lime zest, 1/2 tsp ground cumin, 1/2 tsp smoked paprika, 1/4 tsp chili powder, salt, black pepper, wooden skewers (soaked in water).

Directions:

Preheat the electric smoker to 225°F. In a bowl, whisk together honey, lime juice, soy sauce, olive oil, lime zest, cumin, smoked paprika, chili powder, salt, and black pepper to create the marinade. Thread the salmon cubes onto the soaked wooden skewers. Place the skewers on the smoker racks and brush them with the marinade. Smoke for 30-35 minutes or until the salmon is cooked through and flakes easily.

Smoked Cajun Catfish Po' Boy

Ingredients:

4 catfish fillets, 1/2 cup buttermilk, 1 tbsp Cajun seasoning, 1 tsp paprika, 1/2 tsp garlic powder, 1/2 tsp onion powder, 1/4 tsp cayenne pepper, salt, black pepper, 4 French bread rolls, shredded lettuce, sliced tomatoes, sliced pickles, mayonnaise.

Directions:

Preheat the electric smoker to 250°F. In a shallow dish, combine buttermilk, Cajun seasoning, paprika, garlic powder, onion powder, cayenne pepper, salt, and black pepper. Place the catfish fillets in the dish and let them marinate for 30 minutes. Remove the fillets from the marinade and place them on the smoker racks. Smoke for 20-25 minutes or until the catfish is cooked through and flakes easily. Toast the French bread rolls. Spread mayonnaise on each roll and layer with smoked catfish, shredded lettuce, sliced tomatoes, and sliced pickles.

Soy Ginger Glazed Smoked Mahi-Mahi

Ingredients:

4 mahi-mahi fillets, 1/4 cup soy sauce, 2 tbsp honey, 1 tbsp grated ginger, 2 cloves garlic (minced), 1 tbsp sesame oil, 1 tbsp rice vinegar, 1 tsp cornstarch, 1/4 cup water, sliced green onions for garnish.

Directions:

Preheat the electric smoker to 275°F. In a small saucepan, combine soy sauce, honey, grated ginger, minced garlic, sesame oil, rice vinegar, cornstarch, and water. Cook over medium heat until the mixture thickens slightly. Brush the glaze onto the mahi-mahi fil lets and place them on the smoker racks. Smoke for 20-25 minutes or until the fish is cooked through and flakes easily. Brush the fillets with additional glaze during the smoking process. Once done, garnish with sliced green onions and serve.

Smoked Brown Butter Scallops with Sage

Ingredients:

1 lb sea scallops, 4 tbsp unsalted butter, 8 fresh sage leaves, juice of 1 lemon, salt, black pepper.

Directions:

Preheat the electric smoker to 225°F. In a small saucepan, melt the butter over medium heat and cook until it turns golden brown and gives off a nutty aroma. Remove from heat and add the sage leaves to infuse the butter. Season the scallops with salt and black pepper. Place the scallops on the smoker racks and brush them with the brown butter. Smoke for 20-25 minutes or until the scallops are opaque and cooked through. Drizzle with lemon juice before serving.

Smoked Coconut Curry Shrimp

Ingredients:

1 lb large shrimp, peeled and deveined, 1 cup coconut milk, 2 tbsp red curry paste, 1 tbsp fish sauce, 1 tbsp lime juice, 1 tbsp brown sugar, 1 tsp grated ginger, 2 cloves garlic (minced), chopped fresh cilantro for garnish.

Directions:

Preheat the electric smoker to 250°F. In a bowl, whisk together coconut milk, red curry paste, fish sauce, lime juice, brown sugar, grated ginger, and minced garlic. Add the shrimp to the bowl and toss to coat. Place the shrimp in a smoker tray or on skewers. Smoke for 20-25 minutes or until the shrimp are pink and cooked through. Garnish with chopped cilantro and serve.

Sesame Crusted Smoked Ahi Tuna

Ingredients:

2 ahi tuna steaks, 2 tbsp soy sauce, 1 tbsp sesame oil, 1 tbsp honey, 1 tbsp sesame seeds, salt, black pepper.

Directions:

Preheat the electric smoker to 275°F. In a small bowl, whisk together soy sauce, sesame oil, honey, sesame seeds, salt, and black pepper. Coat the tuna steaks with the mixture. Place the steaks on the smoker racks and smoke for 20-25 minutes or until the tuna is cooked to your desired level of doneness. Let the steaks rest for a few minutes before slicing and serving.

Smoked Lemon Butter Garlic Shrimp Pasta

Ingredients:

1 lb large shrimp, peeled and deveined, 8 oz linguine pasta, 4 tbsp unsalted butter, 4 cloves garlic (minced), juice of 1 lemon, zest of 1 lemon, chopped fresh parsley, salt, black pepper, grated Parmesan cheese for serving.

Directions:

Preheat the electric smoker to 250°F. In a pot of boiling salted water, cook the linguine according to package instructions until al dente. In the meantime, place the shrimp on the smoker racks and smoke for 15-20 minutes or until they are pink and cooked through. In a skillet, melt the butter over medium heat. Add the minced garlic and cook until fragrant. Stir in the lemon juice, lemon zest, chopped parsley, salt, and black pepper. Drain the cooked linguine and toss it in the lemon butter garlic sauce. Add the smoked shrimp and toss to combine. Serve with grated Parmesan cheese on top.

Smoked Teriyaki Salmon Poke Bowl

Ingredients:

4 salmon fillets, 1/4 cup soy sauce, 2 tbsp honey, 1 tbsp rice vinegar, 1 tbsp sesame oil, 1

Directions:

Preheat the electric smoker to 225°F. In a bowl, whisk together soy sauce, honey, rice vinegar, sesame oil, grated ginger, and sliced green onions to create the teriyaki marinade. Place the salmon fillets in the marinade and let them sit for 30 minutes. Remove the salmon from the marinade and place them on the smoker racks. Smoke for 1 hour or until the salmon is cooked through and flakes easily. Remove from the smoker and let it cool slightly. In a bowl, combine cooked sushi rice, sliced avocado, and sliced cucumber. Divide the rice mixture into serving bowls. Top with smoked teriyaki salmon and sprinkle with sesame seeds. Serve as a delicious poke bowl.

Smoked Lemon Herb Butter Lobster

Ingredients:

4 lobster tails, 4 tbsp unsalted butter, 2 cloves garlic (minced), juice of 1 lemon, zest of 1 lemon, 2 tbsp chopped fresh parsley, salt, black pepper.

Directions:

Preheat the electric smoker to 250°F. Using kitchen shears, cut through the top shell of the lobster tails lengthwise. Carefully loosen the meat from the shell, keeping it attached at the base. In a small saucepan, melt the butter over medium heat. Add minced garlic, lemon juice, lemon zest, chopped parsley, salt, and black pepper. Stir until well combined. Brush the lemon herb butter mixture onto the exposed lobster meat. Place the lobster tails on the smoker racks with the meat side up. Smoke for 40-45 minutes or until the meat is opaque and tender. Remove from the smoker and serve hot with additional lemon herb butter on the side.

Smoked Shrimp and Chorizo Paella

Ingredients:

1 lb large shrimp, peeled and deveined, 8 oz chorizo sausage (sliced), 1 onion (chopped), 1 red bell pepper (diced), 2 cloves garlic (minced), 1 cup Arborio rice, 2 cups chicken broth, 1 tsp smoked paprika, 1/2 tsp saffron threads, salt, black pepper, chopped fresh parsley for garnish.

Directions:

Preheat the electric smoker to 275°F. In a skillet, cook the chorizo slices until browned. Remove the chorizo from the skillet and set aside. In the same skillet, sauté the onion, red bell pepper, and minced garlic until softened. Add the Arborio rice and stir to coat with the vegetables. Pour in the chicken broth and add the smoked paprika, saffron threads, salt, and black pepper. Stir well to combine. Place the mixture in a smoker tray or a heat-resistant dish. Add the smoked chorizo and shrimp on top. Smoke for 30-35 minutes or until the rice is cooked and the shrimp are pink and cooked through. Remove from the smoker and garnish with chopped parsley before serving.

Smoked Garlic Herb Butter Scallops

Ingredients:

1 lb sea scallops, 4 tbsp unsalted butter, 4 cloves garlic (minced), 2 tbsp chopped fresh herbs (such as parsley, thyme, and rosemary), juice of 1 lemon, salt, black pepper.

Directions:

Preheat the electric smoker to 225°F. In a small saucepan, melt the butter over medium heat. Add minced garlic and chopped fresh herbs to the melted butter, stirring well. Place the scallops on the smoker racks and brush them generously with the garlic herb butter mixture. Smoke the scallops for 20-25 minutes or until they are opaque and cooked through. Remove from the smoker and squeeze fresh lemon juice over the scallops. Season with salt and black pepper to taste. Serve immediately as a flavorful appetizer or main dish.

Smoked Cajun Stuffed Flounder

Ingredients:

4 flounder fillets, 1 cup cooked crab meat, 1/4 cup breadcrumbs, 2 green onions (chopped), 1/4 cup chopped bell pepper, 1/4 cup mayonnaise, 1 tbsp Cajun seasoning, 1 tbsp fresh lemon juice, salt, black pepper.

Directions:

Preheat the electric smoker to 250°F. In a bowl, combine cooked crab meat, breadcrumbs, chopped green onions, chopped bell pepper, mayonnaise, Cajun seasoning, and fresh lemon juice. Season with salt and black pepper to taste. Lay the flounder fillets flat and spoon the crab mixture onto each fillet. Roll up the fillets and secure them with toothpicks. Place the stuffed flounder on the smoker racks. Smoke for 25-30 minutes or until the fish is cooked through and flakes easily. Remove the toothpicks before serving.

Smoked Maple Glazed Bacon-Wrapped Scallops

Ingredients:

1 lb sea scallops, 8 slices bacon, 1/4 cup maple syrup, 1 tbsp Dijon mustard, 1 tsp soy sauce, 1/2 tsp smoked paprika, salt, black pepper.

Directions:

Preheat the electric smoker to 225°F. Wrap each sea scallop with a slice of bacon and secure with a toothpick. In a small bowl, whisk together maple syrup, Dijon mustard, soy sauce, smoked paprika, salt, and black pepper. Brush the maple glaze onto the bacon-wrapped scallops. Place the scallops on the smoker racks. Smoke for 30-35 minutes or until the bacon is crispy and the scallops are cooked through. Remove the toothpicks before serving.

Smoked Herb-Marinated Mussels

Ingredients:

2 lbs mussels, cleaned and debearded, 1/4 cup olive oil, 2 tbsp chopped fresh herbs (such as parsley, basil, and thyme), 2 cloves garlic (minced), juice of 1 lemon, salt, black pepper.

Directions:

Preheat the electric smoker to 250°F. In a bowl, combine olive oil, chopped fresh herbs, minced garlic, lemon juice, salt, and black pepper. Add the cleaned mussels to the bowl and toss to coat them in the herb marinade. Place the mussels in a smoker tray or a large foil packet. Smoke for 15-20 minutes or until the mussels open and are cooked through. Discard any unopened mussels before serving. Serve the smoked mussels as an appetizer or over pasta.

Smoked Szechuan Pepper Shrimp

Ingredients:

1 lb large shrimp, 2 tbsp Szechuan peppercorns (crushed), 1 tbsp soy sauce, 1 tbsp honey, 1 tbsp rice vinegar, 1 tbsp sesame oil, 1 tsp grated ginger, 2 cloves garlic (minced), sliced green onions for garnish.

Directions:

Preheat the electric smoker to 250°F. In a bowl, combine crushed Szechuan peppercorns, soy sauce, honey, rice vinegar, sesame oil, grated ginger, and minced garlic. Add the shrimp to the bowl and toss to coat them in the marinade. Skewer the shrimp or place them in a smoker tray. Smoke for 20-25 minutes or until the shrimp are pink and cooked through. Remove from the smoker and garnish with sliced green onions. Serve the smoked Szechuan pepper shrimp as an appetizer or as part of a stir-fry or noodle dish.

Smoked Lemon Garlic Butter Clams

Ingredients:

2 lbs clams, 4 tbsp unsalted butter, 4 cloves garlic (minced), zest of 1 lemon, juice of 1 lemon, chopped fresh parsley, salt, black pepper.

Directions:

Preheat the electric smoker to 225°F. In a small saucepan, melt the butter over medium heat. Add minced garlic, lemon zest, lemon juice, chopped parsley, salt, and black pepper to the melted butter, stirring well. Rinse the clams thoroughly and discard any that are open or broken. Place the clams on the smoker racks and brush them with the lemon garlic butter mixture. Smoke for 15-20 minutes or until the clams have opened and are cooked through. Discard any unopened clams before serving.

Smoked Asian Sesame Salmon

Ingredients:

4 salmon fillets, 2 tbsp soy sauce, 1 tbsp sesame oil, 1 tbsp honey, 1 tbsp rice vinegar, 1 tsp grated ginger, 2 cloves garlic (minced), 1 tbsp sesame seeds, sliced green onions for garnish.

Directions:

Preheat the electric smoker to 275°F. In a bowl, whisk together soy sauce, sesame oil, honey, rice vinegar, grated ginger, minced garlic, and sesame seeds. Place the salmon fillets on the smoker racks and brush them with the marinade. Smoke for 20-25 minutes or until the salmon is cooked to your desired level of doneness. Garnish with sliced green onions before serving.

Smoked Brown Sugar Glazed Shrimp Skewers

Ingredients:
1 lb large shrimp, 1/4 cup brown sugar, 2 tbsp olive oil, 2 tbsp soy sauce, 2 tbsp lemon juice, 1 tbsp Dijon mustard, 1 tsp smoked paprika, salt, black pepper.

Directions:
Preheat the electric smoker to 250°F. In a bowl, whisk together brown sugar, olive oil, soy sauce, lemon juice, Dijon mustard, smoked paprika, salt, and black pepper. Skewer the shrimp and place them on the smoker racks. Brush the brown sugar glaze onto the shrimp. Smoke for 15-20 minutes or until the shrimp are pink and cooked through. Baste with additional glaze while smoking if desired.

Smoked Lemon Herb Butter Oysters

Ingredients:
12 oysters, 4 tbsp unsalted butter, 2 cloves garlic (minced), zest of 1 lemon, juice of 1 lemon, 2 tbsp chopped fresh herbs (such as parsley and chives), salt, black pepper.

Directions:
Preheat the electric smoker to 225°F. Shuck the oysters, discarding the top shell and loosening the meat from the bottom shell. In a small saucepan, melt the butter over medium heat. Add minced garlic, lemon zest, lemon juice, chopped herbs, salt, and black pepper to the melted butter, stirring well. Brush the lemon herb butter mixture onto the oysters. Place the oysters on the smoker racks and smoke for 10-15 minutes or until the oysters are cooked through. Remove from the smoker and serve hot.

Smoked Chipotle Lime Buttered Lobster Tails

Ingredients:
4 lobster tails, 4 tbsp unsalted butter, 2 chipotle peppers in adobo sauce (minced), zest of 1 lime, juice of 1 lime, salt, black pepper.

Directions:
Preheat the electric smoker to 250°F. Using kitchen shears, carefully cut through the top shell of each lobster tail lengthwise. Loosen the meat from the shell, keeping it attached at the base. In a small bowl, combine softened butter, minced chipotle peppers, lime zest, lime juice, salt, and black pepper. Spread the chipotle lime butter mixture onto the exposed lobster meat. Place the lobster tails on the smoker racks with the meat side up. Smoke for 40-45 minutes or until the meat is opaque and cooked through. Remove from the smoker and serve hot.

Smoked Garlic Parmesan Halibut

Ingredients:
4 halibut fillets, 4 tbsp grated Parmesan cheese, 2 tbsp olive oil, 2 cloves garlic (minced), 1 tsp dried oregano, 1/2 tsp dried thyme, 1/2 tsp paprika, salt, black pepper.

Directions:
Preheat the electric smoker to 225°F. In a small bowl, combine grated Parmesan cheese, olive oil, minced garlic, dried oregano, dried thyme, paprika, salt, and black pepper. Rub the mixture onto the

halibut fillets, ensuring they are evenly coated. Place the fillets on the smoker racks and smoke for 1 hour or until the fish flakes easily with a fork. Remove from the smoker and serve hot.

Smoked Citrus Soy Glazed Tuna

Ingredients:

2 tuna steaks, 1/4 cup soy sauce, 2 tbsp orange juice, 2 tbsp lime juice, 1 tbsp honey, 1 tsp grated ginger, 2 cloves garlic (minced), 1 tbsp sesame oil, sliced green onions for garnish.

Directions:

Preheat the electric smoker to 275°F. In a bowl, whisk together soy sauce, orange juice, lime juice, honey, grated ginger, minced garlic, and sesame oil. Place the tuna steaks in the marinade and let them marinate for 30 minutes. Remove the tuna from the marinade and place them on the smoker racks. Smoke for 20-25 minutes or until the tuna is cooked to your desired level of doneness. Garnish with sliced green onions before serving.

Smoked Cajun Garlic Butter Shrimp Skewers

Ingredients:

1 lb large shrimp, 4 tbsp unsalted butter, 2 cloves garlic (minced), 1 tbsp Cajun seasoning, 1 tbsp chopped fresh parsley, juice of 1 lemon, salt, black pepper.

Directions:

Preheat the electric smoker to 250°F. Skewer the shrimp and set aside. In a small saucepan, melt the butter over medium heat. Add minced garlic, Cajun seasoning, chopped parsley, lemon juice, salt, and black pepper to the melted butter, stirring well. Brush the Cajun garlic butter mixture onto the shrimp skewers. Place the skewers on the smoker racks and smoke for 15-20 minutes or until the shrimp are pink and cooked through. Baste with additional sauce while smoking if desired. Serve hot.

Smoked Brown Sugar Glazed Rainbow Trout

Ingredients:

4 rainbow trout fillets, 1/4 cup brown sugar, 2 tbsp Dijon mustard, 2 tbsp soy sauce, 1 tbsp apple cider vinegar, 1 tsp smoked paprika, salt, black pepper.

Directions:

Preheat the electric smoker to 225°F. In a small bowl, whisk together brown sugar, Dijon mustard, soy sauce, apple cider vinegar, smoked paprika, salt, and black pepper to create the glaze. Place the rainbow trout fillets on the smoker racks and brush them generously with the brown sugar glaze. Smoke the fillets for 1 hour or until the fish is cooked through and flakes easily. Baste the fillets with the glaze during the smoking process to enhance the flavor. Once done, remove from the smoker and serve hot.

Smoked Ginger Soy Scallops

Ingredients:

1 lb sea scallops, 1/4 cup soy sauce, 2 tbsp honey, 1 tbsp grated ginger, 1 tbsp rice vinegar, 1 tbsp sesame oil, 2 cloves garlic (minced), sliced green onions for garnish.

Directions:

Preheat the electric smoker to 225°F. In a bowl, whisk together soy sauce, honey, grated ginger, rice vinegar, sesame oil, and minced garlic. Add the scallops to the bowl and toss to coat them in the marinade. Place the scallops on the smoker racks and smoke for 20-25 minutes or until they are opaque and cooked through. Remove from the smoker and garnish with sliced green onions. Serve as a delectable appetizer or a main course.

CHAPTER 8: CHEESE AND NUTS RECIPES

Smoked Gouda and Walnut Stuffed Mushrooms
Ingredients:
12 large mushrooms, 4 oz smoked Gouda cheese (grated), 1/4 cup chopped walnuts, 2 tbsp olive oil, 1 tsp dried thyme, 1/2 tsp garlic powder, salt, black pepper.
Directions:
Preheat the electric smoker to 250°F. Remove the stems from the mushrooms and set aside. In a bowl, combine grated smoked Gouda cheese, chopped walnuts, olive oil, dried thyme, garlic powder, salt, and black pepper. Stuff each mushroom cap with the cheese and walnut mixture. Place the stuffed mushrooms on the smoker racks. Smoke for 30-35 minutes or until the cheese is melted and the mushrooms are tender. Serve as a flavorful appetizer.

Smoked Brie with Cranberry Pecan Topping
Ingredients:
1 wheel of Brie cheese, 1/4 cup dried cranberries, 1/4 cup chopped pecans, 2 tbsp honey, 1 tsp balsamic vinegar.
Directions:
Preheat the electric smoker to 225°F. Place the wheel of Brie cheese on a sheet of aluminum foil. In a bowl, combine dried cranberries, chopped pecans, honey, and balsamic vinegar. Spread the cranberry pecan topping over the Brie cheese. Wrap the cheese tightly in the foil, leaving some space for the smoke to circulate. Place the wrapped Brie cheese on the smoker racks. Smoke for 30-35 minutes or until the cheese is soft and gooey. Serve with crackers or bread as a delightful appetizer.

Smoked Cheddar and Rosemary Crackers
Ingredients:
8 oz sharp cheddar cheese (grated), 1 cup all-purpose flour, 1/4 cup unsalted butter (cold and cubed), 1 tbsp chopped fresh rosemary, 1/2 tsp salt, 1/4 tsp black pepper, 2-3 tbsp ice water.
Directions:
Preheat the electric smoker to 275°F. In a food processor, combine grated sharp cheddar cheese, all-purpose flour, cold cubed butter, chopped fresh rosemary, salt, and black pepper. Pulse until the mixture resembles coarse crumbs. Gradually add ice water, 1 tbsp at a time, and pulse until the dough comes together. Roll out the dough on a floured surface and cut into desired cracker shapes. Place the crackers on a baking sheet or smoker tray. Smoke for 15-20 minutes or until the crackers are golden and crisp. Let them cool before serving.

Smoked Blue Cheese and Pecan Dip
Ingredients:
8 oz cream cheese, 4 oz blue cheese (crumbled), 1/2 cup chopped pecans, 1/4 cup mayonnaise, 2 tbsp sour cream, 1 tbsp chopped fresh chives, 1 tsp Worcestershire sauce, 1/2 tsp garlic powder, salt, black pepper.
Directions:

Preheat the electric smoker to 250°F. In a bowl, combine cream cheese, crumbled blue cheese, chopped pecans, mayonnaise, sour cream, chopped fresh chives, Worcestershire sauce, garlic powder, salt, and black pepper. Mix until well combined. Transfer the mixture to a heat-resistant dish. Place the dish on the smoker racks. Smoke for 30-35 minutes or until the dip is heated through and the flavors are melded. Stir the dip before serving. Serve with crackers, bread, or vegetable sticks.

Smoked Gruyere Cheese and Walnut Stuffed Peppers

Ingredients:
4 bell peppers (any color), 8 oz Gruyere cheese (grated), 1/2 cup chopped walnuts, 2 tbsp olive oil, 1 tsp dried thyme, 1/2 tsp garlic powder, salt, black pepper.

Directions:
Preheat the electric smoker to 250°F. Slice off the tops of the bell peppers and remove the seeds and membranes. In a bowl, combine grated Gruyere cheese, chopped walnuts, olive oil, dried thyme, garlic powder, salt, and black pepper. Stuff each bell pepper with the cheese and walnut mixture. Place the stuffed bell peppers on the smoker racks. Smoke for 40-45 minutes or until the peppers are tender and the cheese is melted and bubbly. Serve as a delicious and savory side dish.

Smoked Parmesan and Herb Almonds

Ingredients:
2 cups whole almonds, 1/4 cup grated Parmesan cheese, 2 tbsp olive oil, 1 tbsp chopped fresh herbs (such as rosemary, thyme, or oregano), 1/2 tsp garlic powder, 1/2 tsp salt.

Directions:
Preheat the electric smoker to 225°F. In a bowl, combine whole almonds, grated Parmesan cheese, olive oil, chopped fresh herbs, garlic powder, and salt. Toss until the almonds are evenly coated. Spread the almonds in a single layer on a smoker tray or a baking sheet. Smoke for 1 hour, stirring occasionally, until the almonds are toasted and fragrant. Allow them to cool before serving as a tasty snack or appetizer.

Smoked Camembert with Maple Pecan Drizzle

Ingredients:
1 wheel of Camembert cheese, 1/4 cup chopped pecans, 2 tbsp maple syrup, 1 tbsp unsalted butter.

Directions:
Preheat the electric smoker to 250°F. Place the wheel of Camembert cheese on a sheet of aluminum foil. In a small saucepan, melt the butter over low heat. Add chopped pecans and maple syrup, stirring well to coat the pecans. Pour the maple pecan mixture over the Camembert cheese. Wrap the cheese tightly in the foil, leaving some space for the smoke to circulate. Place the wrapped Camembert cheese on the smoker racks. Smoke for 30-35 minutes or until the cheese is soft and gooey. Serve with crusty bread or crackers as a delectable appetizer.

Smoked Feta and Olive Stuffed Mushrooms

Ingredients:
12 large mushrooms, 4 oz feta cheese (crumbled), 1/4 cup chopped Kalamata olives, 2 tbsp olive oil, 1 tsp dried oregano, 1/2 tsp garlic powder, salt, black pepper.

Directions:

Preheat the electric smoker to 250°F. Remove the stems from the mushrooms and set aside. In a bowl, combine crumbled feta cheese, chopped Kalamata olives, olive oil, dried oregano, garlic powder, salt, and black pepper. Stuff each mushroom cap with the feta and olive mixture. Place the stuffed mushrooms on the smoker racks. Smoke for 30-35 minutes or until the cheese is soft and the mushrooms are tender. Serve as a flavorful appetizer or side dish.

Smoked Cheddar and Rosemary Biscuits

Ingredients:

2 cups all-purpose flour, 1 tbsp baking powder, 1/2 tsp salt, 1/2 tsp garlic powder, 1/2 tsp dried rosemary, 1/2 cup unsalted butter (cold and cubed), 1 cup shredded sharp cheddar cheese, 3/4 cup buttermilk.

Directions:

Preheat the electric smoker to 375°F. In a large bowl, whisk together all-purpose flour, baking powder, salt, garlic powder, and dried rosemary. Add the cold cubed butter to the bowl and use a pastry cutter or your fingers to cut the butter into the flour mixture until it resembles coarse crumbs. Stir in the shredded cheddar cheese. Gradually add the buttermilk, mixing until the dough comes together. Turn the dough out onto a floured surface and knead it gently for a minute. Roll out the dough to about 1/2-inch thickness and cut out biscuits using a round biscuit cutter. Place the biscuits on a baking sheet or smoker tray. Smoke for 15-20 minutes or until the biscuits are golden brown and cooked through. Serve warm as a delightful accompaniment to any meal.

Smoked Goat Cheese and Pistachio Salad

Ingredients:

6 cups mixed salad greens, 4 oz goat cheese (crumbled), 1/2 cup roasted pistachios (chopped), 1/4 cup dried cranberries, 2 tbsp balsamic vinegar, 2 tbsp extra-virgin olive oil, 1 tsp Dijon mustard, salt, black pepper.

Directions:

Preheat the electric smoker to 250°F. In a large bowl, combine mixed salad greens, crumbled goat cheese, chopped pistachios, and dried cranberries. In a separate small bowl, whisk together balsamic vinegar, olive oil, Dijon mustard, salt, and black pepper to create the dressing. Drizzle the dressing over the salad mixture and toss until well coated. Place the salad in a smoker tray or a large foil packet. Smoke for 10-15 minutes or until the flavors are infused and the salad greens are slightly wilted. Serve as a refreshing and satisfying salad.

Smoked Blue Cheese and Walnut Crostini

Ingredients:

1 baguette, 4 oz blue cheese (crumbled), 1/2 cup chopped walnuts, 2 tbsp honey, fresh thyme leaves for garnish.

Directions:

Preheat the electric smoker to 250°F. Slice the baguette into thin slices and arrange them on a baking sheet or smoker tray. Toast the slices in the smoker for 10-12 minutes or until they are crisp and lightly golden. Remove from the smoker and let them cool slightly. In a bowl, combine crumbled blue cheese, chopped walnuts, and honey. Spread the blue cheese and walnut mixture onto the toasted baguette slices. Place the crostini back on the smoker racks. Smoke for an additional 5-7 minutes or until the cheese is melted and the flavors meld together. Remove from the smoker and garnish with fresh thyme leaves. Serve as an elegant appetizer or party snack.

Smoked Mozzarella and Tomato Bruschetta
Ingredients:
1 baguette, 8 oz smoked mozzarella cheese (sliced), 2 large tomatoes (sliced), 1/4 cup fresh basil leaves, 2 tbsp balsamic glaze, salt, black pepper.
Directions:
Preheat the electric smoker to 250°F. Slice the baguette into thick slices and arrange them on a baking sheet or smoker tray. Toast the slices in the smoker for 10-12 minutes or until they are crisp and lightly golden. Remove from the smoker and let them cool slightly. On each slice of toasted baguette, layer a slice of smoked mozzarella cheese, a tomato slice, and a fresh basil leaf. Drizzle with balsamic glaze and season with salt and black pepper to taste. Place the bruschetta back on the smoker racks. Smoke for an additional 5-7 minutes or until the cheese is melted and the flavors meld together. Remove from the smoker and serve as a delightful appetizer or light lunch.

Smoked Pepper Jack and Jalapeño Poppers
Ingredients:
12 jalapeño peppers, 8 oz cream cheese, 4 oz shredded pepper jack cheese, 12 slices bacon, salt, black pepper.
Directions:
Preheat the electric smoker to 250°F. Slice each jalapeño pepper in half lengthwise and remove the seeds and membranes. In a bowl, combine cream cheese, shredded pepper jack cheese, salt, and black pepper. Fill each jalapeño half with the cheese mixture. Wrap each jalapeño popper with a slice of bacon and secure with a toothpick. Place the poppers on the smoker racks. Smoke for 30-35 minutes or until the bacon is crispy and the peppers are tender. Remove the toothpicks before serving.

Smoked Gorgonzola and Walnut Salad
Ingredients:
6 cups mixed salad greens, 4 oz Gorgonzola cheese (crumbled), 1 cup toasted walnuts, 1/2 cup dried cranberries, 2 tbsp red wine vinegar, 2 tbsp extra-virgin olive oil, 1 tsp Dijon mustard, salt, black pepper.
Directions:
Preheat the electric smoker to 250°F. In a large bowl, combine mixed salad greens, crumbled Gorgonzola cheese, toasted walnuts, and dried cranberries. In a separate small bowl, whisk together red wine vinegar, olive oil, Dijon mustard, salt, and black pepper to create the dressing. Drizzle the dressing over the salad mixture and toss until well coated. Place the salad in a smoker tray or a large foil packet. Smoke for 10-15 minutes or until the flavors are infused and the salad greens are slightly wilted. Serve as a flavorful and satisfying salad.

Smoked Swiss Cheese and Ham Roll-Ups
Ingredients:

8 slices Swiss cheese, 8 slices deli ham, 1/4 cup Dijon mustard, 1 tbsp honey, fresh dill sprigs for garnish.

Directions:

Preheat the electric smoker to 250°F. Lay a slice of Swiss cheese on top of a slice of deli ham. Spread a thin layer of Dijon mustard on the cheese. Drizzle honey over the mustard. Roll up the cheese and ham tightly and secure with toothpicks. Place the roll-ups on the smoker racks. Smoke for 15-20 minutes or until the cheese is melted and the flavors are blended. Remove the toothpicks before serving. Garnish with fresh dill sprigs for added freshness.

Smoked Cheddar and Bacon Stuffed Potatoes

Ingredients:

4 large baking potatoes, 4 oz shredded cheddar cheese, 4 slices cooked bacon (crumbled), 2 tbsp sour cream, 2 tbsp chopped chives, salt, black pepper.

Directions:

Preheat the electric smoker to 250°F. Scrub the baking potatoes clean and pierce them several times with a fork. Place the potatoes directly on the smoker racks. Smoke for 1-1.5 hours or until the potatoes are tender. Remove the potatoes from the smoker and let them cool slightly. Cut each potato in half lengthwise and scoop out the flesh, leaving a thin layer to create potato shells. In a bowl, combine the scooped potato flesh with shredded cheddar cheese, crumbled bacon, sour cream, chopped chives, salt, and black pepper. Spoon the mixture back into the potato shells. Place the potato halves back on the smoker racks. Smoke for an additional 15-20 minutes or until the cheese is melted and bubbly. Remove from the smoker and serve as a satisfying side dish or appetizer.

Smoked Havarti and Cranberry Grilled Cheese

Ingredients:

8 slices bread of your choice, 8 oz sliced Havarti cheese, 1/2 cup dried cranberries, 2 tbsp unsalted butter.

Directions:

Preheat the electric smoker to 250°F. Assemble the sandwiches by placing Havarti cheese slices and dried cranberries between two slices of bread. Spread butter on the outer sides of each sandwich. Place the sandwiches on the smoker racks. Smoke for 10-12 minutes on each side or until the cheese is melted and the bread is toasted. Remove from the smoker and slice the sandwiches. Serve as a delightful and unique twist on a classic grilled cheese.

Smoked Gouda and Pecan Stuffed Dates

Ingredients:

12 Medjool dates, 4 oz smoked Gouda cheese (cut into small cubes), 1/4 cup chopped pecans, 2 tbsp honey, fresh thyme leaves for garnish.

Directions:

Preheat the electric smoker to 250°F. Make a lengthwise slit in each date and remove the pit. Stuff each date with a cube of smoked Gouda cheese and a sprinkle of chopped pecans. Place the stuffed dates on the smoker racks. Smoke for 15-20 minutes or until the cheese is melted and the dates are softened. Remove from the smoker and drizzle with honey. Garnish with fresh thyme leaves. Serve as a sweet and savory appetizer or dessert.

Smoked Cheddar and Walnut Scones

Ingredients:

2 cups all-purpose flour, 2 tsps baking powder, 1/2 tsp salt, 1/2 cup unsalted butter (cold and cubed), 1 cup shredded sharp cheddar cheese, 1/2 cup chopped walnuts, 3/4 cup buttermilk.

Directions:

Preheat the electric smoker to 375°F. In a large bowl, whisk together all-purpose flour, baking powder, and salt. Add the cold cubed butter to the bowl and use a pastry cutter or your fingers to cut the butter into the flour mixture until it resembles coarse crumbs. Stir in the shredded cheddar cheese and chopped walnuts. Gradually add the buttermilk, mixing until the dough comes together. Turn the dough out onto a floured surface and knead it gently for a minute. Pat the dough into a circle about 1-inch thick. Cut the dough into wedges and place them on a baking sheet or smoker tray. Smoke for 15-20 minutes or until the scones are golden brown and cooked through. Serve warm as a delightful accompaniment to tea or breakfast.

Smoked Gorgonzola and Pear Salad

Ingredients:

6 cups mixed salad greens, 4 oz crumbled Gorgonzola cheese, 1 ripe pear (thinly sliced), 1/2 cup candied pecans, 2 tbsp balsamic vinegar, 2 tbsp extra-virgin olive oil, 1 tsp honey, salt, black pepper.

Directions:

Preheat the electric smoker to 250°F. In a large bowl, combine mixed salad greens, crumbled Gorgonzola cheese, sliced pear, and candied pecans. In a separate small bowl, whisk together balsamic vinegar, olive oil, honey, salt, and black pepper to create the dressing. Drizzle the dressing over the salad mixture and toss until well coated. Place the salad in a smoker tray or a large foil packet. Smoke for 10-15 minutes or until the flavors are infused and the salad greens are slightly wilted. Serve as a refreshing and flavorful salad.

Smoked Blue Cheese and Walnut Stuffed Chicken Breast

Ingredients:

4 boneless, skinless chicken breasts, 4 oz crumbled blue cheese, 1/2 cup chopped walnuts, 2 tbsp olive oil, 1 tsp dried thyme, 1/2 tsp garlic powder, salt, black pepper.

Directions:

Preheat the electric smoker to 250°F. Slice a pocket into each chicken breast by cutting horizontally through the thickest part of the breast, being careful not to cut all the way through. In a bowl, combine crumbled blue cheese, chopped walnuts, olive oil, dried thyme, garlic powder, salt, and black pepper. Stuff each chicken breast with the blue cheese and walnut mixture. Secure the openings with toothpicks if necessary. Place the stuffed chicken breasts on the smoker racks. Smoke for 45-50 minutes or until the chicken is cooked through and the cheese is melted. Remove the toothpicks before serving.

Smoked Cheddar and Bacon Macaroni and Cheese

Ingredients:

8 oz elbow macaroni, 4 slices cooked bacon (crumbled), 2 tbsp unsalted butter, 2 tbsp all-purpose flour, 2 cups milk, 2 cups shredded sharp cheddar cheese, 1/2 tsp smoked paprika, salt, black pepper.

Directions:

Preheat the electric smoker to 250°F. Cook the elbow macaroni according to the package instructions until al dente. In a large saucepan, melt the butter over medium heat. Stir in the flour and cook for 1-2 minutes until slightly golden. Gradually whisk in the milk and cook, stirring constantly, until the mixture thickens. Remove from heat and stir in the shredded cheddar cheese, crumbled bacon, smoked paprika, salt, and black pepper. Add the cooked macaroni to the cheese sauce and stir until well coated. Transfer the macaroni and cheese mixture to a heat-resistant dish. Place the dish on the smoker racks. Smoke for 20-25 minutes or until the flavors are melded and the top is golden and slightly crispy. Serve as a comforting and cheesy main dish.

Smoked Feta and Spinach Stuffed Mushrooms

Ingredients:

12 large mushrooms, 4 oz crumbled feta cheese, 1 cup chopped spinach, 2 tbsp olive oil, 1 tsp dried oregano, 1/2 tsp garlic powder, salt, black pepper.

Directions:

Preheat the electric smoker to 250°F. Remove the stems from the mushrooms and set aside. In a bowl, combine crumbled feta cheese, chopped spinach, olive oil, dried oregano, garlic powder, salt, and black pepper. Stuff each mushroom cap with the feta and spinach mixture. Place the stuffed mushrooms on the smoker racks. Smoke for 30-35 minutes or until the cheese is melted and the mushrooms are tender. Serve as a flavorful and vegetarian-friendly appetizer or side dish.

Smoked Havarti and Apple Grilled Sandwich

Ingredients:

8 slices bread of your choice, 8 oz sliced Havarti cheese, 1 apple (thinly sliced), 2 tbsp unsalted butter.

Directions:

Preheat the electric smoker to 250°F. Assemble the sandwiches by placing Havarti cheese slices and apple slices between two slices of bread. Spread butter on the outer sides of each sandwich. Place the sandwiches on the smoker racks. Smoke for 10-12 minutes on each side or until the cheese is melted and the bread is toasted. Remove from the smoker and slice the sandwiches. Serve as a delightful and unique twist on a classic grilled cheese.

Smoked Gouda and Fig Crostini

Ingredients:

1 baguette, 8 oz sliced smoked Gouda cheese, 1 cup sliced fresh figs, 2 tbsp honey, fresh thyme leaves for garnish.

Directions: Preheat the electric smoker to 250°F. Slice the baguette into thin slices and arrange them on a baking sheet or smoker tray. Toast the slices in the smoker for 10-12 minutes or until they are crisp and lightly golden. Remove from the smoker and let them cool slightly. On each slice of toasted baguette, layer a slice of smoked Gouda cheese and a few slices of fresh figs. Drizzle with honey and garnish with fresh thyme leaves. Place the crostini back on the smoker racks. Smoke for an additional 5-7 minutes or until the cheese is melted and the flavors meld together. Remove from the smoker and serve as an elegant appetizer or party snack.

Smoked Pecan and Blue Cheese Salad

Ingredients:

6 cups mixed salad greens, 4 oz crumbled blue cheese, 1 cup toasted pecans, 1/2 cup dried cranberries, 2 tbsp red wine vinegar, 2 tbsp extra-virgin olive oil, 1 tsp Dijon mustard, salt, black pepper.

Directions:

Preheat the electric smoker to 250°F. In a large bowl, combine mixed salad greens, crumbled blue cheese, toasted pecans, and dried cranberries. In a separate small bowl, whisk together red wine vinegar, olive oil, Dijon mustard, salt, and black pepper to create the dressing. Drizzle the dressing over the salad mixture and toss until well coated. Place the salad in a smoker tray or a large foil packet. Smoke for 10-15 minutes or until the flavors are infused and the salad greens are slightly wilted. Serve as a flavorful and satisfying salad.

Smoked Pepper Jack and Walnut Stuffed Chicken

Ingredients:

4 boneless, skinless chicken breasts, 4 oz shredded pepper jack cheese, 1/2 cup chopped walnuts, 2 tbsp olive oil, 1 tsp dried thyme, 1/2 tsp garlic powder, salt, black pepper.

Directions:

Preheat the electric smoker to 250°F. Slice a pocket into each chicken breast by cutting horizontally through the thickest part of the breast, being careful not to cut all the way through. In a bowl, combine shredded pepper jack cheese, chopped walnuts, olive oil, dried thyme, garlic powder, salt, and black pepper. Stuff each chicken breast with the cheese and walnut mixture. Secure the openings with toothpicks if necessary. Place the stuffed chicken breasts on the smoker racks. Smoke for 45-50 minutes or until the chicken is cooked through and the cheese is melted. Remove the toothpicks before serving.

Smoked Cheddar and Bacon Cornbread Muffins

Ingredients:

1 cup cornmeal, 1 cup all-purpose flour, 1 tbsp sugar, 2 tsps baking powder, 1/2 tsp salt, 1 cup shredded sharp cheddar cheese, 4 slices cooked bacon (crumbled), 1 cup buttermilk, 1/4 cup unsalted butter (melted), 1/4 cup honey, 2 large eggs.

Directions:

Preheat the electric smoker to 375°F. In a large bowl, whisk together cornmeal, all-purpose flour, sugar, baking powder, and salt. Stir in shredded cheddar cheese and crumbled bacon. In a separate bowl, whisk together buttermilk, melted butter, honey, and eggs. Pour the wet ingredients into the dry ingredients and stir until just combined. Grease a muffin tin or line it with muffin liners. Spoon the batter into the muffin cups, filling each about three-fourths full. Place the muffin tin on the smoker racks. Smoke for 15-18 minutes or until the muffins are golden brown and a toothpick inserted into the center comes out clean. Remove from the smoker and let them cool slightly before serving.

Smoked Feta and Spinach Stuffed Chicken Breast

Ingredients:

4 boneless, skinless chicken breasts, 4 oz crumbled feta cheese, 1 cup chopped spinach, 2 tbsp olive oil, 1 tsp dried oregano, 1/2 tsp garlic powder, salt, black pepper.

Directions:

Preheat the electric smoker to 250°F. Slice a pocket into each chicken breast by cutting horizontally through the thickest part of the breast, being careful not to cut all the way through. In a bowl, combine crumbled feta cheese, chopped spinach, olive oil, dried oregano, garlic powder, salt, and black pepper. Stuff each chicken breast with the feta and spinach mixture. Secure the openings with toothpicks if necessary. Place the stuffed chicken breasts on the smoker racks. Smoke for 45-50 minutes or until the chicken is cooked through and the cheese is melted. Remove the toothpicks before serving.

Smoked Havarti and Pear Grilled Sandwich
Ingredients:
8 slices bread of your choice, 8 oz sliced Havarti cheese, 1 pear (thinly sliced), 2 tbsp unsalted butter.
Directions:
Preheat the electric smoker to 250°F. Assemble the sandwiches by placing Havarti cheese slices and pear slices between two slices of bread. Spread butter on the outer sides of each sandwich. Place the sandwiches on the smoker racks. Smoke for 10-12 minutes on each side or until the cheese is melted and the bread is toasted. Remove from the smoker and slice the sandwiches. Serve as a delightful and unique twist on a classic grilled cheese.

Smoked Gouda and Fig Salad
Ingredients:
6 cups mixed salad greens, 4 oz sliced smoked Gouda cheese, 1 cup sliced fresh figs, 1/2 cup candied pecans, 2 tbsp balsamic vinegar, 2 tbsp extra-virgin olive oil, salt, black pepper.
Directions:
Preheat the electric smoker to 250°F. In a large bowl, combine mixed salad greens, sliced smoked Gouda cheese, sliced fresh figs, and candied pecans. In a separate small bowl, whisk together balsamic vinegar, olive oil, salt, and black pepper to create the dressing. Drizzle the dressing over the salad mixture and toss until well coated. Place the salad in a smoker tray or a large foil packet. Smoke for 10-15 minutes or until the flavors are infused and the salad greens are slightly wilted. Serve as a flavorful and satisfying salad.

Smoked Cheddar and Bacon Stuffed Bell Peppers
Ingredients:
4 bell peppers (any color), 8 oz shredded cheddar cheese, 4 slices cooked bacon (crumbled), 2 tbsp olive oil, 1 tsp dried thyme, 1/2 tsp garlic powder, salt, black pepper.
Directions:
Preheat the electric smoker to 250°F. Slice off the tops of the bell peppers and remove the seeds and membranes. In a bowl, combine shredded cheddar cheese, crumbled bacon, olive oil, dried thyme, garlic powder, salt, and black pepper. Stuff each bell pepper with the cheese and bacon mixture. Place the stuffed bell peppers on the smoker racks. Smoke for 40-45 minutes or until the peppers are tender and the cheese is melted and bubbly. Remove from the smoker and serve as a delicious and savory side dish or main course.

Smoked Blue Cheese and Walnut Dip
Ingredients:
8 oz cream cheese, 4 oz crumbled blue cheese, 1/2 cup chopped walnuts, 1/4 cup mayonnaise, 2 tbsp sour cream, 1 tbsp chopped fresh chives, 1 tsp Worcestershire sauce, 1/2 tsp garlic powder, salt, black pepper.
Directions:
Preheat the electric smoker to 250°F. In a bowl, combine cream cheese, crumbled blue cheese, chopped walnuts, mayonnaise, sour cream, chopped fresh chives, Worcestershire sauce, garlic powder, salt, and

black pepper. Mix until well combined. Transfer the mixture to a heat-resistant dish. Place the dish on the smoker racks. Smoke for 30-35 minutes or until the dip is heated through and the flavors are melded. Stir the dip before serving. Serve with crackers, bread, or vegetable sticks.

Smoked Gruyere and Bacon Quiche
Ingredients:
1 prepared pie crust, 4 oz sliced smoked Gruyere cheese, 4 slices cooked bacon (crumbled), 1/2 cup chopped spinach, 4 large eggs, 1 cup milk, 1/4 tsp dried thyme, salt, black pepper.
Directions:
Preheat the electric smoker to 350°F. Place the prepared pie crust in a pie dish. Layer the smoked Gruyere cheese, crumbled bacon, and chopped spinach in the pie crust. In a separate bowl, whisk together eggs, milk, dried thyme, salt, and black pepper. Pour the egg mixture over the cheese, bacon, and spinach in the pie crust. Place the quiche on the smoker racks. Smoke for 30-35 minutes or until the center is set and the top is golden brown. Remove from the smoker and let it cool slightly before slicing and serving.

Smoked Feta and Olive Dip
Ingredients:
8 oz cream cheese, 4 oz crumbled feta cheese, 1/2 cup chopped Kalamata olives, 1/4 cup chopped fresh parsley, 2 tbsp lemon juice, 2 tbsp extra-virgin olive oil, 1/2 tsp dried oregano, salt, black pepper.
Directions:
Preheat the electric smoker to 250°F. In a bowl, combine cream cheese, crumbled feta cheese, chopped Kalamata olives, chopped fresh parsley, lemon juice, olive oil, dried oregano, salt, and black pepper. Mix until well combined. Transfer the mixture to a heat-resistant dish. Place the dish on the smoker racks. Smoke for 30-35 minutes or until the dip is heated through and the flavors are melded. Stir the dip before serving. Serve with pita bread, crackers, or vegetable sticks.

Smoked Cheddar and Walnut Stuffed Dates
Ingredients:
12 Medjool dates, 4 oz shredded cheddar cheese, 1/4 cup chopped walnuts, 2 tbsp honey, fresh thyme leaves for garnish.
Directions:
Preheat the electric smoker to 250°F. Make a lengthwise slit in each date and remove the pit. Stuff each date with shredded cheddar cheese and a sprinkle of chopped walnuts. Place the stuffed dates on the smoker racks. Smoke for 15-20 minutes or until the cheese is melted and the dates are softened. Remove from the smoker and drizzle with honey. Garnish with fresh thyme leaves. Serve as a sweet and savory appetizer or snack.

Smoked Gouda and Bacon Pasta
Ingredients:
8 oz penne pasta, 4 oz smoked Gouda cheese (shredded), 4 slices cooked bacon (crumbled), 1/2 cup chopped sun-dried tomatoes, 2 tbsp chopped fresh basil, 2 tbsp grated Parmesan cheese, 2 tbsp olive oil, salt, black pepper.
Directions:

Preheat the electric smoker to 250°F. Cook the penne pasta according to the package instructions until al dente. In a large bowl, combine the cooked pasta, shredded smoked Gouda cheese, crumbled bacon, chopped sun-dried tomatoes, chopped fresh basil, grated Parmesan cheese, olive oil, salt, and black pepper. Toss until well combined and the cheese starts to melt. Transfer the pasta mixture to a heat-resistant dish. Place the dish on the smoker racks. Smoke for 20-25 minutes or until the flavors are blended and the cheese is fully melted. Remove from the smoker and serve as a flavorful and comforting pasta dish.

Smoked Blue Cheese and Pear Crostini
Ingredients:
1 baguette, 4 oz crumbled blue cheese, 1 ripe pear (thinly sliced), 2 tbsp honey, fresh thyme leaves for garnish.
Directions:
Preheat the electric smoker to 250°F. Slice the baguette into thin slices and arrange them on a baking sheet or smoker tray. Toast the slices in the smoker for 10-12 minutes or until they are crisp and lightly golden. Remove from the smoker and let them cool slightly. On each slice of toasted baguette, spread a layer of crumbled blue cheese. Top with a slice of pear and drizzle with honey. Garnish with fresh thyme leaves. Place the crostini back on the smoker racks. Smoke for an additional 5-7 minutes or until the cheese is softened and the flavors meld together. Remove from the smoker and serve as an elegant and flavorful appetizer.

Smoked Gruyere and Mushroom Quiche
Ingredients:
1 prepared pie crust, 4 oz sliced smoked Gruyere cheese, 1 cup sliced mushrooms, 1/4 cup chopped fresh chives, 4 large eggs, 1 cup milk, 1/4 tsp dried thyme, salt, black pepper.
Directions:
Preheat the electric smoker to 350°F. Place the prepared pie crust in a pie dish. Layer the smoked Gruyere cheese, sliced mushrooms, and chopped fresh chives in the pie crust. In a separate bowl, whisk together eggs, milk, dried thyme, salt, and black pepper. Pour the egg mixture over the cheese, mushrooms, and chives in the pie crust. Place the quiche on the smoker racks. Smoke for 30-35 minutes or until the center is set and the top is golden brown. Remove from the smoker and let it cool slightly before slicing and serving.

Smoked Feta and Herb Flatbread
Ingredients:
2 cups all-purpose flour, 2 tsps baking powder, 1/2 tsp salt, 1/2 cup plain Greek yogurt, 1/4 cup olive oil, 1/4 cup water, 4 oz crumbled feta cheese, 1 tbsp chopped fresh herbs (such as basil, parsley, or dill), salt, black pepper.
Directions:
Preheat the electric smoker to 400°F. In a large bowl, whisk together all-purpose flour, baking powder, and salt. In a separate bowl, combine Greek yogurt, olive oil, and water. Pour the wet ingredients into the dry ingredients and mix until a dough forms. Knead the dough on a floured surface for a few minutes until it becomes smooth. Roll out the dough into a thin rectangle or circle. Transfer the dough onto a smoker tray or directly onto the smoker racks. Smoke for 10-12 minutes or until the flatbread is

cooked and slightly golden. Remove from the smoker and let it cool slightly. In a bowl, combine crumbled feta cheese, chopped fresh herbs, salt, and black pepper. Sprinkle the feta and herb mixture over the smoked flatbread. Cut into desired shapes and serve as a flavorful appetizer or side dish.

CHAPTER 9: VEGETABLE RECIPES

Smoked Stuffed Bell Peppers
Ingredients:
4 bell peppers (any color), 1 cup cooked quinoa, 1 cup black beans (drained and rinsed), 1 cup diced tomatoes, 1/2 cup corn kernels, 1/2 cup shredded cheddar cheese, 2 tbsp chopped fresh cilantro, 1 tsp cumin, 1/2 tsp chili powder, salt, black pepper.
Directions: Preheat the electric smoker to 250°F. Slice off the tops of the bell peppers and remove the seeds and membranes. In a bowl, combine cooked quinoa, black beans, diced tomatoes, corn kernels, shredded cheddar cheese, chopped fresh cilantro, cumin, chili powder, salt, and black pepper. Stuff each bell pepper with the mixture. Place the stuffed bell peppers on the smoker racks. Smoke for 45-50 minutes or until the peppers are tender and the filling is heated through. Remove from the smoker and serve as a delicious and nutritious main course.

Smoked Zucchini and Mushroom Skewers
Ingredients:
2 zucchini (sliced into rounds), 8 oz mushrooms, 1 red onion (cut into chunks), 2 tbsp olive oil, 2 cloves garlic (minced), 1 tbsp fresh lemon juice, 1 tsp dried oregano, salt, black pepper.
Directions:
Preheat the electric smoker to 250°F. In a bowl, combine zucchini rounds, mushrooms, and red onion chunks. In a separate small bowl, whisk together olive oil, minced garlic, lemon juice, dried oregano, salt, and black pepper. Pour the marinade over the vegetables and toss to coat. Thread the marinated vegetables onto skewers. Place the skewers on the smoker racks. Smoke for 20-25 minutes or until the

vegetables are tender and lightly charred. Remove from the smoker and serve as a flavorful and healthy side dish.

Smoked Sweet Potato Wedges

Ingredients:

2 large sweet potatoes, 2 tbsp olive oil, 1 tsp smoked paprika, 1/2 tsp garlic powder, 1/2 tsp dried thyme, salt, black pepper.

Directions:

Preheat the electric smoker to 250°F. Cut the sweet potatoes into wedges. In a bowl, combine olive oil, smoked paprika, garlic powder, dried thyme, salt, and black pepper. Toss the sweet potato wedges in the seasoned oil mixture until well coated. Place the sweet potato wedges on the smoker racks. Smoke for 30-35 minutes or until the wedges are tender and slightly crispy. Remove from the smoker and serve as a tasty and nutritious side dish.

Smoked Portobello Mushroom Burgers

Ingredients:

4 large portobello mushrooms, 4 burger buns, 4 slices Swiss cheese, 4 tbsp balsamic glaze, 2 tbsp olive oil, 2 cloves garlic (minced), 1 tsp dried rosemary, salt, black pepper.

Directions:

Preheat the electric smoker to 250°F. Remove the stems from the portobello mushrooms. In a bowl, combine olive oil, minced garlic, dried rosemary, salt, and black pepper. Brush the seasoned oil mixture onto both sides of the portobello mushrooms. Place the mushrooms on the smoker racks. Smoke for 25-30 minutes or until the mushrooms are tender and juicy. During the last few minutes of smoking, place a slice of Swiss cheese on each mushroom to melt. Remove from the smoker and assemble the burgers by placing each smoked portobello mushroom on a burger bun. Drizzle with balsamic glaze and serve as a satisfying vegetarian option.

Smoked Cauliflower Steaks

Ingredients:

1 head cauliflower, 2 tbsp olive oil, 1 tsp smoked paprika, 1/2 tsp garlic powder, 1/2 tsp dried thyme, salt, black pepper.

Directions:

Preheat the electric smoker to 250°F. Slice the cauliflower into thick steaks, about 1-inch thick. In a bowl, combine olive oil, smoked paprika, garlic powder, dried thyme, salt, and black pepper. Brush both sides of the cauliflower steaks with the seasoned oil mixture. Place the cauliflower steaks on the smoker racks. Smoke for 30-35 minutes or until the steaks are tender and lightly charred. Remove from the smoker and serve as a flavorful and hearty vegetable main dish or side.

Smoked Ratatouille

Ingredients:

1 eggplant, 1 zucchini, 1 yellow squash, 1 red bell pepper, 1 yellow bell pepper, 1 onion, 2 cloves garlic, 3 tbsp olive oil, 1 tbsp tomato paste, 1 tsp dried thyme, 1 tsp dried basil, salt, black pepper.

Directions:

Preheat the electric smoker to 250°F. Cut the eggplant, zucchini, yellow squash, red bell pepper, yellow bell pepper, and onion into bite-sized chunks. Mince the garlic cloves. In a large bowl, combine the chopped vegetables and minced garlic. Drizzle with olive oil and sprinkle with tomato paste, dried thyme, dried basil, salt, and black pepper. Toss to coat the vegetables evenly. Place the seasoned vegetables in a smoker tray or large foil packet. Smoke for 45-50 minutes or until the vegetables are tender and infused with smoky flavor. Remove from the smoker and serve as a delicious and colorful vegetable medley.

Smoked Broccoli and Cauliflower Salad

Ingredients:

2 cups broccoli florets, 2 cups cauliflower florets, 1/4 cup sliced almonds, 1/4 cup dried cranberries, 2 tbsp lemon juice, 2 tbsp extra-virgin olive oil, 1 tsp Dijon mustard, salt, black pepper.

Directions:

Preheat the electric smoker to 250°F. In a large bowl, combine broccoli florets, cauliflower florets, sliced almonds, and dried cranberries. In a separate small bowl, whisk together lemon juice, olive oil, Dijon mustard, salt, and black pepper to create the dressing. Drizzle the dressing over the salad mixture and toss until well coated. Place the salad in a smoker tray or a large foil packet. Smoke for 10-15 minutes or until the flavors are infused and the vegetables are slightly tender. Serve as a refreshing and nutritious salad.

Smoked Stuffed Mushrooms

Ingredients:

12 large mushrooms, 1 cup breadcrumbs, 1/2 cup grated Parmesan cheese, 1/4 cup chopped fresh parsley, 2 tbsp olive oil, 2 cloves garlic (minced), 1 tsp dried oregano, salt, black pepper.

Directions:

Preheat the electric smoker to 250°F. Remove the stems from the mushrooms and set aside. In a bowl, combine breadcrumbs, grated Parmesan cheese, chopped fresh parsley, olive oil, minced garlic, dried oregano, salt, and black pepper. Stuff each mushroom cap with the breadcrumb mixture. Place the stuffed mushrooms on the smoker racks. Smoke for 20-25 minutes or until the mushrooms are tender and the filling is golden brown. Remove from the smoker and serve as a flavorful and satisfying appetizer or side dish.

Smoked Brussels Sprouts with Bacon

Ingredients:

1 lb Brussels sprouts, 2 tbsp olive oil, 4 slices cooked bacon (crumbled), 2 cloves garlic (minced), 1 tsp smoked paprika, salt, black pepper.

Directions:

Preheat the electric smoker to 250°F. Trim the ends of the Brussels sprouts and remove any outer leaves. Cut larger sprouts in half. In a bowl, combine Brussels sprouts, olive oil, crumbled bacon, minced garlic, smoked paprika, salt, and black pepper. Toss to coat the sprouts evenly. Place the seasoned Brussels sprouts in a smoker tray or large foil packet. Smoke for 30-35 minutes or until the sprouts are tender and lightly charred. Remove from the smoker and serve as a flavorful and smoky side dish.

Smoked Stuffed Tomatoes

Ingredients:

4 large tomatoes, 1 cup cooked quinoa, 1/2 cup crumbled feta cheese, 1/4 cup chopped fresh basil, 2 tbsp chopped sun-dried tomatoes, 1 tbsp balsamic vinegar, 2 cloves garlic (minced), 2 tbsp olive oil, salt, black pepper.

Directions:

Preheat the electric smoker to 250°F. Cut off the tops of the tomatoes and scoop out the seeds and pulp. In a bowl, combine cooked quinoa, crumbled feta cheese, chopped fresh basil, chopped sun-dried tomatoes, balsamic vinegar, minced garlic, olive oil, salt, and black pepper. Stuff each tomato with the quinoa mixture. Place the stuffed tomatoes on the smoker racks. Smoke for 20-25 minutes or until the tomatoes are tender and the filling is heated through. Remove from the smoker and serve as a flavorful and healthy appetizer or side dish.

Smoked Corn on the Cob with Herb Butter

Ingredients:

4 ears of corn, 4 tbsp unsalted butter (softened), 2 tbsp chopped fresh herbs (such as parsley, basil, or chives), 1 tsp smoked paprika, salt, black pepper.

Directions:

Preheat the electric smoker to 250°F. Peel back the husks of the corn, leaving them attached at the base. Remove the silk threads from the corn and fold the husks back into place. In a bowl, combine softened butter, chopped fresh herbs, smoked paprika, salt, and black pepper. Gently pull back the husks of the corn and spread the herb butter over the kernels. Fold the husks back into place. Place the corn on the smoker racks. Smoke for 20-25 minutes or until the corn is tender and lightly charred. Remove from the smoker and let it cool slightly before serving.

Smoked Roasted Root Vegetables

Ingredients:

2 carrots (peeled and cut into sticks), 2 parsnips (peeled and cut into sticks), 1 sweet potato (peeled and cut into chunks), 1 red onion (cut into wedges), 2 tbsp olive oil, 1 tsp dried rosemary, 1/2 tsp garlic powder, salt, black pepper.

Directions:

Preheat the electric smoker to 250°F. In a large bowl, combine carrot sticks, parsnip sticks, sweet potato chunks, and red onion wedges. Drizzle with olive oil and sprinkle with dried rosemary, garlic powder, salt, and black pepper. Toss to coat the vegetables evenly. Place the seasoned vegetables in a smoker tray or large foil packet. Smoke for 45-50 minutes or until the vegetables are tender and slightly caramelized. Remove from the smoker and serve as a flavorful and nutritious side dish.

Smoked Stuffed Eggplant

Ingredients:

2 small eggplants, 1 cup cooked quinoa, 1/2 cup diced tomatoes, 1/2 cup crumbled feta cheese, 1/4 cup chopped fresh parsley, 2 tbsp chopped Kalamata olives, 2 cloves garlic (minced), 2 tbsp olive oil, 1 tsp dried oregano, salt, black pepper.

Directions:

Preheat the electric smoker to 250°F. Cut the eggplants in half lengthwise and scoop out the flesh, leaving a 1/4-inch thick shell. In a bowl, combine cooked quinoa, diced tomatoes, crumbled feta cheese, chopped fresh parsley, chopped Kalamata olives, minced garlic, olive oil, dried oregano, salt, and black pepper. Fill the eggplant shells with the quinoa mixture. Place the stuffed eggplants on the smoker racks. Smoke for 30-35 minutes or until the eggplants are tender and the filling is heated through. Remove from the smoker and serve as a flavorful and satisfying vegetarian main dish.

Smoked Vegetable Stir-Fry
Ingredients:
2 cups mixed vegetables (such as broccoli florets, bell peppers, snap peas, and carrots), 1 cup sliced mushrooms, 1/2 cup sliced red onion, 2 cloves garlic (minced), 2 tbsp soy sauce, 1 tbsp honey, 1 tsp sesame oil, 1/2 tsp grated ginger, 2 tbsp olive oil, salt, black pepper.
Directions:
Preheat the electric smoker to 250°F. In a bowl, combine mixed vegetables, sliced mushrooms, sliced red onion, minced garlic, soy sauce, honey, sesame oil, olive oil, salt, and black pepper. Toss to coat the vegetables evenly. Place the seasoned vegetables in a smoker tray or large foil packet. Smoke for 15-20 minutes or until the vegetables are tender-crisp and infused with smoky flavor. Remove from the smoker and serve as a flavorful and healthy stir-fry.

Smoked Asparagus with Lemon Butter
Ingredients:
1 bunch asparagus, 2 tbsp unsalted butter (melted), 1 tbsp fresh lemon juice, 1 tsp lemon zest, salt, black pepper.
Directions:
Preheat the electric smoker to 250°F. Trim the woody ends of the asparagus spears. In a small bowl, combine melted butter, lemon juice, lemon zest, salt, and black pepper. Drizzle the lemon butter mixture over the asparagus and toss to coat. Place the asparagus on the smoker racks. Smoke for 10-12 minutes or until the asparagus is tender yet still crisp. Remove from the smoker and serve as a vibrant and flavorful side dish.

Smoked Stuffed Portobello Mushrooms
Ingredients:
4 large portobello mushrooms, 1 cup cooked quinoa, 1/2 cup chopped sun-dried tomatoes, 1/4 cup crumbled goat cheese, 2 tbsp chopped fresh basil, 1 tbsp balsamic vinegar, 2 cloves garlic (minced), 2 tbsp olive oil, salt, black pepper.
Directions:
Preheat the electric smoker to 250°F. Remove the stems from the portobello mushrooms. In a bowl, combine cooked quinoa, chopped sun-dried tomatoes, crumbled goat cheese, chopped fresh basil, minced garlic, balsamic vinegar, olive oil, salt, and black pepper. Stuff each portobello mushroom with the quinoa mixture. Place the stuffed mushrooms on the smoker racks. Smoke for 20-25 minutes or until the mushrooms are tender and the filling is heated through. Remove from the smoker and serve as a flavorful and satisfying appetizer or main dish.

**Smoked Caprese Salad
Ingredients:
4 large tomatoes, 8 oz fresh mozzarella cheese (sliced), 1 cup fresh basil leaves, 2 tbsp balsamic glaze, 2 tbsp extra-virgin olive oil, salt, black pepper.
Directions:

Preheat the electric smoker to 250°F. Slice the tomatoes and fresh mozzarella cheese into thick rounds. On a serving platter, layer the tomato slices, mozzarella slices, and fresh basil leaves. Drizzle with balsamic glaze and olive oil. Season with salt and black pepper to taste. Place the platter in the smoker. Smoke for 10-12 minutes or until the flavors are infused and the cheese softens slightly. Remove from the smoker and serve as a delightful and refreshing salad.

Smoked Vegetable Kabobs
Ingredients:
2 zucchini (cut into thick rounds), 2 yellow squash (cut into thick rounds), 1 red bell pepper (cut into chunks), 1 yellow bell pepper (cut into chunks), 1 red onion (cut into wedges), 8 cherry tomatoes, 2 tbsp olive oil, 2 cloves garlic (minced), 1 tsp dried thyme, 1 tsp dried oregano, salt, black pepper.
Directions:
Preheat the electric smoker to 250°F. Thread the zucchini rounds, yellow squash rounds, red bell pepper chunks, yellow bell pepper chunks, red onion wedges, and cherry tomatoes onto skewers, alternating the vegetables. In a bowl, combine olive oil, minced garlic, dried thyme, dried oregano, salt, and black pepper. Brush the seasoned oil mixture onto the vegetable kabobs. Place the kabobs on the smoker racks. Smoke for 20-25 minutes or until the vegetables are tender and lightly charred. Remove from the smoker and serve as a flavorful and colorful dish.

Smoked Stuffed Artichokes
Ingredients:
4 large artichokes, 1 cup breadcrumbs, 1/2 cup grated Parmesan cheese, 1/4 cup chopped fresh parsley, 2 cloves garlic (minced), 2 tbsp lemon juice, 2 tbsp olive oil, salt, black pepper.
Directions:
Preheat the electric smoker to 250°F. Trim the tops and stems of the artichokes. Cut off the sharp tips of the leaves. In a bowl, combine breadcrumbs, grated Parmesan cheese, chopped fresh parsley, minced garlic, lemon juice, olive oil, salt, and black pepper. Stuff the breadcrumb mixture between the leaves of each artichoke. Place the stuffed artichokes on the smoker racks. Smoke for 45-50 minutes or until the artichokes are tender and the breadcrumbs are golden brown. Remove from the smoker and serve as a flavorful and unique appetizer or side dish.

Smoked Veggie Pizza
Ingredients:
1 prepared pizza dough, 1/2 cup tomato sauce, 1 cup shredded mozzarella cheese, 1 cup sliced mushrooms, 1/2 cup sliced bell peppers, 1/2 cup sliced red onions, 1/4 cup sliced black olives, 2 tbsp chopped fresh basil, 1 tbsp olive oil, salt, black pepper.
Directions:
Preheat the electric smoker to 400°F. Roll out the pizza dough into your desired shape and thickness. Place the dough on a pizza stone or a baking sheet. Spread tomato sauce evenly over the dough, leaving a border for the crust. Sprinkle shredded mozzarella cheese over the sauce. Arrange sliced mushrooms, bell peppers, red onions, and black olives over the cheese. Drizzle with olive oil and season with salt and black pepper. Place the pizza in the smoker. Smoke for 15-18 minutes or until the crust is golden brown and the cheese is melted and bubbly. Remove from the smoker and sprinkle with chopped fresh basil. Let it cool slightly before slicing and serving as a delicious and smoky vegetable pizza.

Smoked Butternut Squash Soup

Ingredients:

1 butternut squash (peeled, seeded, and cubed), 1 onion (chopped), 2 cloves garlic (minced), 4 cups vegetable broth, 1/2 cup coconut milk, 1 tsp dried sage, 1/2 tsp ground cinnamon, salt, black pepper.

Directions:

Preheat the electric smoker to 250°F. Place the cubed butternut squash, chopped onion, and minced garlic in a smoker-safe pot or baking dish. Pour the vegetable broth over the vegetables. Cover the pot with a lid or foil. Place the pot on the smoker racks. Smoke for 1-1.5 hours or until the squash is tender and easily mashed. Remove from the smoker and let it cool slightly. Using an immersion blender or regular blender, puree the smoked vegetables and broth until smooth. Return the soup to a pot and stir in coconut milk, dried sage, ground cinnamon, salt, and black pepper. Heat the soup on the stovetop until warmed through. Serve hot as a comforting and flavorful soup.

Smoked Ratatouille Stuffed Mushrooms

Ingredients:

12 large mushrooms, 1 cup diced eggplant, 1 cup diced zucchini, 1 cup diced bell peppers, 1 cup diced tomatoes, 1/4 cup chopped fresh basil, 2 tbsp olive oil, 2 cloves garlic (minced), salt, black pepper.

Directions:

Preheat the electric smoker to 250°F. Remove the stems from the mushrooms and set aside. In a bowl, combine diced eggplant, diced zucchini, diced bell peppers, diced tomatoes, chopped fresh basil, minced garlic, olive oil, salt, and black pepper. Stuff each mushroom cap with the ratatouille mixture. Place the stuffed mushrooms on the smoker racks. Smoke for 20-25 minutes or until the mushrooms are tender and the filling is cooked through. Remove from the smoker and serve as a flavorful and vegetable-packed appetizer or side dish.

Smoked Vegetable Frittata

Ingredients:

8 large eggs, 1/4 cup milk, 1 cup diced bell peppers, 1 cup diced zucchini, 1/2 cup diced red onion, 1/2 cup sliced cherry tomatoes, 1/4 cup grated Parmesan cheese, 2 tbsp chopped fresh parsley, 1 tbsp olive oil, salt, black pepper.

Directions:

Preheat the electric smoker to 350°F. In a bowl, whisk together eggs and milk. Stir in diced bell peppers, diced zucchini, diced red onion, sliced cherry tomatoes, grated Parmesan cheese, chopped fresh parsley, salt, and black pepper. Heat olive oil in an oven-safe skillet over medium heat. Pour the egg mixture into the skillet. Place the skillet on the smoker racks. Smoke for 20-25 minutes or until the frittata is set and lightly golden on top. Remove from the smoker and let it cool slightly before slicing and serving as a flavorful and protein-rich breakfast or brunch option.

Smoked Stuffed Cabbage Rolls

Ingredients:

8 large cabbage leaves, 1 cup cooked quinoa, 1 cup diced mushrooms, 1/2 cup diced onions, 1/2 cup diced carrots, 1/4 cup tomato sauce, 2 tbsp chopped fresh dill, 1 tbsp olive oil, 1 tsp smoked paprika, salt, black pepper.

Directions:

Preheat the electric smoker to 250°F. Bring a pot of water to a boil and blanch the cabbage leaves for 2-3 minutes until they are pliable. Remove from the water and pat dry with a paper towel. In a bowl, combine cooked quinoa, diced mushrooms, diced onions, diced carrots, tomato sauce, chopped fresh dill, olive oil, smoked paprika, salt, and black pepper. Place a portion of the filling onto each cabbage leaf and roll it tightly, tucking in the sides as you go. Secure the rolls with toothpicks if necessary. Place the stuffed cabbage rolls on the smoker racks. Smoke for 45-50 minutes or until the cabbage is tender and the filling is heated through. Remove from the smoker and let them cool slightly before serving as a flavorful and satisfying main dish.

Smoked Garlic and Herb Roasted Vegetables

Ingredients:
2 cups mixed root vegetables (such as potatoes, carrots, and parsnips), 1 cup Brussels sprouts, 1 cup cauliflower florets, 4 cloves garlic (minced), 2 tbsp olive oil, 1 tbsp chopped fresh rosemary, 1 tbsp chopped fresh thyme, salt, black pepper.

Directions:
Preheat the electric smoker to 250°F. Cut the root vegetables into bite-sized chunks. In a large bowl, combine mixed root vegetables, Brussels sprouts, cauliflower florets, minced garlic, olive oil, chopped fresh rosemary, chopped fresh thyme, salt, and black pepper. Toss to coat the vegetables evenly. Place the seasoned vegetables in a smoker tray or large foil packet. Smoke for 45-50 minutes or until the vegetables are tender and golden brown. Remove from the smoker and serve as a delicious and aromatic roasted vegetable medley.

Smoked Quinoa Stuffed Bell Peppers

Ingredients:
4 bell peppers (any color), 1 cup cooked quinoa, 1 cup diced tomatoes, 1/2 cup corn kernels, 1/2 cup black beans (drained and rinsed), 1/4 cup diced red onion, 2 tbsp chopped fresh cilantro, 1 tbsp lime juice, 1 tsp ground cumin, salt, black pepper.

Directions:
Preheat the electric smoker to 250°F. Slice off the tops of the bell peppers and remove the seeds and membranes. In a bowl, combine cooked quinoa, diced tomatoes, corn kernels, black beans, diced red onion, chopped fresh cilantro, lime juice, ground cumin, salt, and black pepper. Stuff each bell pepper with the quinoa mixture. Place the stuffed bell peppers on the smoker racks. Smoke for 40-45 minutes or until the peppers are tender and the filling is heated through. Remove from the smoker and serve as a nutritious and flavorful main course.

Smoked Roasted Vegetable Salad

Ingredients:
2 cups mixed roasted vegetables (such as eggplant, zucchini, bell peppers, and cherry tomatoes), 4 cups mixed salad greens, 1/4 cup crumbled feta cheese, 2 tbsp balsamic vinegar, 2 tbsp extra-virgin olive oil, 1 tbsp honey, salt, black pepper.

Directions:
Preheat the electric smoker to 250°F. Toss the mixed roasted vegetables in a bowl with a drizzle of olive oil, salt, and black pepper. Place the vegetables on the smoker racks. Smoke for 10-15 minutes or until they are heated through and infused with smoky flavor. In a separate bowl, combine balsamic vinegar,

olive oil, honey, salt, and black pepper to create the dressing. Place the salad greens in a serving bowl and top with the smoked roasted vegetables. Sprinkle crumbled feta cheese over the salad. Drizzle the balsamic dressing over the top. Toss gently to combine. Serve the smoked roasted vegetable salad as a flavorful and nutritious side dish or light lunch option.

Smoked Stuffed Portobello Mushrooms with Quinoa and Spinach

Ingredients:

4 large portobello mushrooms, 1 cup cooked quinoa, 1 cup chopped spinach, 1/2 cup diced red bell pepper, 1/4 cup chopped red onion, 2 cloves garlic (minced), 2 tbsp grated Parmesan cheese, 2 tbsp olive oil, 1 tbsp balsamic vinegar, salt, black pepper.

Directions:

Preheat the electric smoker to 250°F. Remove the stems from the portobello mushrooms. In a bowl, combine cooked quinoa, chopped spinach, diced red bell pepper, chopped red onion, minced garlic, grated Parmesan cheese, olive oil, balsamic vinegar, salt, and black pepper. Stuff each portobello mushroom cap with the quinoa mixture. Place the stuffed mushrooms on the smoker racks. Smoke for 20-25 minutes or until the mushrooms are tender and the filling is heated through. Remove from the smoker and serve as a flavorful and protein-packed vegetarian main dish.

Smoked Roasted Beet Salad

Ingredients:

4 beets (peeled and cut into wedges), 4 cups mixed salad greens, 1/4 cup crumbled goat cheese, 1/4 cup chopped walnuts, 2 tbsp balsamic vinegar, 2 tbsp extra-virgin olive oil, 1 tbsp honey, salt, black pepper.

Directions:

Preheat the electric smoker to 250°F. Toss the beet wedges in a bowl with a drizzle of olive oil, salt, and black pepper. Place the beets on the smoker racks. Smoke for 30-35 minutes or until the beets are tender. In a separate bowl, whisk together balsamic vinegar, olive oil, honey, salt, and black pepper to create the dressing. Arrange the mixed salad greens on serving plates. Top with the smoked roasted beets, crumbled goat cheese, and chopped walnuts. Drizzle the balsamic dressing over the salad. Serve as a vibrant and flavorful salad option.

Smoked Stuffed Acorn Squash

Ingredients:

2 acorn squash, 1 cup cooked wild rice, 1/2 cup diced apples, 1/4 cup dried cranberries, 1/4 cup chopped pecans, 2 tbsp maple syrup, 2 tbsp unsalted butter (melted), 1 tsp ground cinnamon, salt, black pepper.

Directions:

Preheat the electric smoker to 250°F. Cut the acorn squash in half and remove the seeds. In a bowl, combine cooked wild rice, diced apples, dried cranberries, chopped pecans, maple syrup, melted butter, ground cinnamon, salt, and black pepper. Fill each acorn squash half with the wild rice mixture. Place the stuffed squash on the smoker racks. Smoke for 40-45 minutes or until the squash is tender and the filling is heated through. Remove from the smoker and let it cool slightly before serving as a comforting and flavorful side dish.

Smoked Bruschetta

Ingredients:

4 slices of crusty bread, 2 large tomatoes (diced), 1/4 cup chopped fresh basil, 2 tbsp balsamic vinegar, 2 tbsp extra-virgin olive oil, 2 cloves garlic (minced), salt, black pepper.

Directions:

Preheat the electric smoker to 250°F. Place the bread slices on the smoker racks. Smoke for 5-7 minutes or until the bread is slightly toasted and infused with smoky flavor. In a bowl, combine diced tomatoes, chopped fresh basil, balsamic vinegar, olive oil, minced garlic, salt, and black pepper. Remove the bread slices from the smoker and top each slice with the tomato mixture. Serve the smoked bruschetta as a flavorful and appetizing appetizer or light snack.

Smoked Stuffed Peppers with Lentils and Vegetables

Ingredients:

4 bell peppers (any color), 1 cup cooked lentils, 1 cup diced zucchini, 1/2 cup diced carrots, 1/2 cup diced celery, 1/4 cup diced red onion, 2 cloves garlic (minced), 2 tbsp tomato paste, 2 tbsp chopped fresh parsley, 1 tbsp olive oil, 1 tsp dried oregano, salt, black pepper.

Directions:

Preheat the electric smoker to 250°F. Slice off the tops of the bell peppers and remove the seeds and membranes. In a bowl, combine cooked lentils, diced zucchini, diced carrots, diced celery, diced red onion, minced garlic, tomato paste, chopped fresh parsley, olive oil, dried oregano, salt, and black pepper. Stuff each bell pepper with the lentil and vegetable mixture. Place the stuffed peppers on the smoker racks. Smoke for 40-45 minutes or until the peppers are tender and the filling is heated through. Remove from the smoker and serve as a nutritious and satisfying vegetarian main course.

Smoked Sweet Potato and Kale Hash

Ingredients:

2 sweet potatoes (peeled and diced), 2 cups chopped kale, 1 red bell pepper (diced), 1/2 red onion (diced), 2 cloves garlic (minced), 2 tbsp olive oil, 1 tsp smoked paprika, 1/2 tsp ground cumin, salt, black pepper.

Directions:

Preheat the electric smoker to 250°F. In a bowl, combine diced sweet potatoes, chopped kale, diced red bell pepper, diced red onion, minced garlic, olive oil, smoked paprika, ground cumin, salt, and black pepper. Toss to coat the ingredients evenly. Place the sweet potato and kale mixture in a smoker tray or large foil packet. Smoke for 30-35 minutes or until the sweet potatoes are tender and lightly caramelized. Remove from the smoker and serve as a flavorful and nutritious side dish or breakfast hash.

Smoked Cauliflower and Chickpea Curry

Ingredients:

1 head cauliflower (cut into florets), 1 can chickpeas (drained and rinsed), 1 onion (chopped), 2 cloves garlic (minced), 1 tbsp grated ginger, 1 can coconut milk, 2 tbsp tomato paste, 1 tbsp curry powder, 1 tsp ground cumin, 1 tsp ground coriander, salt, black pepper.

Directions:

Preheat the electric smoker to 250°F. Place the cauliflower florets, chickpeas, chopped onion, minced garlic, and grated ginger in a smoker-safe pot or baking dish. In a separate bowl, whisk together coconut milk, tomato paste, curry powder, ground cumin, ground coriander, salt, and black pepper. Pour the coconut milk mixture over the vegetables. Cover the pot with a lid or foil. Place the pot on the smoker racks. Smoke for 1-1.5 hours or until the cauliflower is tender and the flavors have melded together. Remove from the smoker and serve the smoked cauliflower and chickpea curry over steamed rice or with naan bread for a satisfying and aromatic meal.

Smoked Spinach and Mushroom Quesadilla
Ingredients:
4 large tortillas, 2 cups sliced mushrooms, 2 cups fresh spinach, 1 cup shredded mozzarella cheese, 1/2 cup diced red onion, 2 cloves garlic (minced), 2 tbsp olive oil, salt, black pepper.
Directions:
Preheat the electric smoker to 250°F. In a skillet, heat olive oil over medium heat. Add sliced mushrooms, diced red onion, and minced garlic. Cook until the mushrooms are tender and the onions are translucent. Add fresh spinach to the skillet and cook until wilted. Season with salt and black pepper to taste. Place a tortilla on the smoker racks. Spread a layer of the mushroom and spinach mixture over half of the tortilla. Sprinkle shredded mozzarella cheese over the vegetables. Fold the tortilla in half to form a quesadilla. Repeat with the remaining tortillas and filling. Smoke the quesadillas for 5-7 minutes on each side or until the tortillas are crispy and the cheese is melted. Remove from the smoker and let them cool slightly before slicing into wedges. Serve the smoked spinach and mushroom quesadillas as a flavorful and satisfying meal.

Smoked Ratatouille Pizza
Ingredients:
1 prepared pizza dough, 1/2 cup tomato sauce, 1 cup shredded mozzarella cheese, 1 cup diced eggplant, 1 cup diced zucchini, 1 cup diced bell peppers, 1/2 cup sliced red onion, 2 cloves garlic (minced), 2 tbsp olive oil, 2 tbsp chopped fresh basil, salt, black pepper.
Directions:
Preheat the electric smoker to 400°F. Roll out the pizza dough into your desired shape and thickness. Place the dough on a pizza stone or a baking sheet. Spread tomato sauce evenly over the dough, leaving a border for the crust. Sprinkle shredded mozzarella cheese over the sauce. In a bowl, combine diced eggplant, diced zucchini, diced bell peppers, sliced red onion, minced garlic, olive oil, chopped fresh basil, salt, and black pepper. Toss to coat the vegetables evenly. Arrange the vegetable mixture on top of the cheese. Place the pizza in the smoker. Smoke for 15-18 minutes or until the crust is golden brown and the cheese is melted and bubbly. Remove from the smoker and let it cool slightly before slicing and serving as a flavorful and smoky pizza.

Smoked Veggie Tacos
Ingredients:
8 small tortillas, 2 cups sliced bell peppers (any color), 1 cup sliced zucchini, 1 cup sliced yellow squash, 1/2 cup sliced red onion, 2 cloves garlic (minced), 2 tbsp olive oil, 1 tsp chili powder, 1/2 tsp ground cumin, 1/2 tsp smoked paprika, salt, black pepper.
Directions:
Preheat the electric smoker to 250°F. In a bowl, combine sliced bell peppers, sliced zucchini, sliced yellow squash, sliced red onion, minced garlic, olive oil, chili powder, ground cumin, smoked paprika,

salt, and black pepper. Toss to coat the vegetables evenly. Place the seasoned vegetables in a smoker tray or large foil packet. Smoke for 15-20 minutes or until the vegetables are tender and lightly charred. Warm the tortillas on the smoker racks for a few minutes. Remove the tortillas and spoon the smoked vegetables onto each tortilla. Serve the smoked veggie tacos with your favorite toppings such as salsa, guacamole, or sour cream for a delicious and satisfying meal.

Smoked Stuffed Portobello Mushroom Caps
Ingredients:
4 large portobello mushroom caps, 1 cup cooked quinoa, 1 cup chopped baby spinach, 1/2 cup diced tomatoes, 1/4 cup crumbled feta cheese, 2 tbsp chopped fresh parsley, 2 tbsp balsamic glaze, 2 tbsp olive oil, salt, black pepper.
Directions: Preheat the electric smoker to 250°F. Remove the stems from the portobello mushroom caps and gently scrape out the gills using a spoon. In a bowl, combine cooked quinoa, chopped baby spinach, diced tomatoes, crumbled feta cheese, chopped fresh parsley, balsamic glaze, olive oil, salt, and black pepper. Spoon the quinoa mixture into each mushroom cap, filling it generously. Place the stuffed mushroom caps on the smoker racks. Smoke for 20-25 minutes or until the mushrooms are tender and the filling is heated through. Remove from the smoker and let them cool slightly before serving as a flavorful and satisfying appetizer or main dish.

Smoked Vegetable Spring Rolls
Ingredients:
8 rice paper wrappers, 2 cups julienned mixed vegetables (such as carrots, cucumbers, bell peppers, and lettuce), 1 cup cooked rice noodles, 1/4 cup chopped fresh mint leaves, 1/4 cup chopped fresh cilantro leaves, 2 tbsp soy sauce, 1 tbsp rice vinegar, 1 tbsp honey, 1 tsp grated ginger, 1 tsp sesame oil.
Directions:
Preheat the electric smoker to 250°F. Fill a shallow dish with warm water. Dip one rice paper wrapper into the water for a few seconds until it becomes pliable. Place the wet rice paper on a clean surface. Arrange a small portion of the julienned vegetables, rice noodles, fresh mint leaves, and fresh cilantro leaves in the center of the rice paper. Fold the sides of the wrapper over the filling, then roll it tightly to form a spring roll. Repeat with the remaining rice paper wrappers and filling. In a small bowl, whisk together soy sauce, rice vinegar, honey, grated ginger, and sesame oil to create the dipping sauce. Place the spring rolls on the smoker racks. Smoke for 5-7 minutes or until the wrappers are slightly crisp. Remove from the smoker and serve the smoked vegetable spring rolls with the dipping sauce for a light and flavorful appetizer or snack.

Smoked Mediterranean Veggie Skewers
Ingredients:
8 wooden skewers, 2 cups cubed eggplant, 2 cups cherry tomatoes, 1 cup sliced red onion, 1 cup sliced bell peppers (any color), 1/4 cup chopped fresh parsley, 2 tbsp olive oil, 2 tbsp lemon juice, 2 cloves garlic (minced), 1 tsp dried oregano, salt, black pepper.
Directions:
Preheat the electric smoker to 250°F. Soak the wooden skewers in water for about 30 minutes to prevent them from burning. Thread the cubed eggplant, cherry tomatoes, sliced red onion, and sliced bell peppers onto the skewers, alternating the vegetables. In a bowl, combine chopped fresh parsley, olive

oil, lemon juice, minced garlic, dried oregano, salt, and black pepper. Brush the seasoned oil mixture over the vegetable skewers. Place the skewers on the smoker racks. Smoke for 15-20 minutes or until the vegetables are tender and lightly charred. Remove from the smoker and serve the smoked Mediterranean veggie skewers as a flavorful and colorful appetizer or side dish.

CHAPTER 10: SAUCE AND RUBS RECIPES

Sweet Honey BBQ Sauce
Ingredients:
1 cup ketchup, ½ cup honey, ¼ cup apple cider vinegar, 2 tbsp Worcestershire sauce, 1 tbsp brown sugar, 1 tsp garlic powder, 1 tsp onion powder, salt and pepper to taste.
Directions:
In a saucepan, combine all the ingredients over medium heat. Bring to a simmer and cook for 10 minutes, stirring occasionally. Let cool before using. Brush onto your smoked meats during the last 10 minutes of cooking.

Spicy Chipotle Rub
Ingredients:
2 tbsp chipotle powder, 1 tbsp paprika, 1 tbsp brown sugar, 1 tsp garlic powder, 1 tsp onion powder, 1 tsp cumin, 1 tsp salt, ½ tsp black pepper.
Directions:
In a bowl, mix all the ingredients until well combined. Generously rub onto your meat before smoking. Smoke at a temperature of 225°F for the recommended cooking time.

Tangy Mustard BBQ Sauce
Ingredients:
1 cup yellow mustard, ½ cup apple cider vinegar, ¼ cup honey, 2 tbsp ketchup, 2 tbsp Worcestershire sauce, 1 tsp garlic powder, 1 tsp onion powder, salt and pepper to taste.
Directions:
In a saucepan, whisk together all the ingredients over medium heat. Bring to a simmer and cook for 5 minutes, stirring constantly. Allow the sauce to cool before serving. Brush onto your smoked meats during the last 10 minutes of cooking.

Savory Herb Rub
Ingredients:
2 tbsp dried thyme, 2 tbsp dried rosemary, 1 tbsp dried oregano, 1 tbsp garlic powder, 1 tbsp onion powder, 1 tsp paprika, 1 tsp salt, ½ tsp black pepper.
Directions:
In a small bowl, combine all the ingredients thoroughly. Rub the mixture generously onto your meat before placing it in the smoker. Smoke at a temperature of 250°F until the meat reaches the desired internal temperature.

Sweet and Smoky BBQ Sauce
Ingredients:
1 cup ketchup, ½ cup brown sugar, ¼ cup apple cider vinegar, 2 tbsp molasses, 1 tbsp Worcestershire sauce, 1 tbsp smoked paprika, 1 tsp garlic powder, 1 tsp onion powder, salt and pepper to taste.
Directions:

In a saucepan, combine all the ingredients over medium heat. Simmer for 10 minutes, stirring occasionally. Allow the sauce to cool before using. Brush onto your smoked meats during the last 10 minutes of cooking.

Citrus Herb Rub

Ingredients:

2 tbsp dried thyme, 2 tbsp dried rosemary, 2 tbsp dried parsley, 1 tbsp lemon zest, 1 tbsp orange zest, 1 tsp garlic powder, 1 tsp onion powder, salt and pepper to taste.

Directions:

In a bowl, combine dried thyme, dried rosemary, dried parsley, lemon zest, orange zest, garlic powder, onion powder, salt, and pepper. Mix well to ensure even distribution of flavors. Generously rub the mixture onto your meat before placing it in the electric smoker. Smoke at the recommended temperature until the meat reaches the desired doneness.

Kansas City Style BBQ Sauce

Ingredients:

1 cup ketchup, ½ cup brown sugar, ¼ cup apple cider vinegar, 2 tbsp molasses, 1 tbsp Worcestershire sauce, 1 tbsp onion powder, 1 tbsp garlic powder, 1 tsp smoked paprika, ½ tsp black pepper, salt to taste.

Directions:

In a saucepan, combine all the ingredients over medium heat. Bring to a simmer and cook for 15 minutes, stirring occasionally. Allow the sauce to cool before using. Brush onto your smoked meats during the last 10 minutes of cooking.

Coffee Cocoa Rub

Ingredients:

2 tbsp ground coffee, 2 tbsp cocoa powder, 1 tbsp brown sugar, 1 tsp chili powder, 1 tsp garlic powder, 1 tsp salt, ½ tsp black pepper.

Directions:

In a bowl, mix all the ingredients until well combined. Generously rub onto your meat before smoking. Smoke at a temperature of 225°F for the recommended cooking time.

Carolina Gold BBQ Sauce

Ingredients:

1 cup yellow mustard, ½ cup apple cider vinegar, ¼ cup honey, 2 tbsp ketchup, 1 tbsp Worcestershire sauce, 1 tbsp brown sugar, 1 tsp garlic powder, 1 tsp onion powder, 1 tsp hot sauce, salt and pepper to taste.

Directions:

In a saucepan, whisk together all the ingredients over medium heat. Simmer for 10 minutes, stirring constantly. Allow the sauce to cool before serving. Brush onto your smoked meats during the last 10 minutes of cooking.

Spicy Cajun Rub

Ingredients:

2 tbsp paprika, 1 tbsp garlic powder, 1 tbsp onion powder, 1 tbsp dried oregano, 1 tbsp dried thyme, 1 tbsp cayenne pepper, 1 tsp salt, ½ tsp black pepper.

Directions:

In a small bowl, combine all the ingredients thoroughly. Rub the mixture generously onto your meat before placing it in the smoker. Smoke at a temperature of 250°F until the meat reaches the desired internal temperature.

Sweet and Tangy Pineapple BBQ Sauce

Ingredients:

1 cup pineapple juice, ½ cup ketchup, ¼ cup brown sugar, 2 tbsp soy sauce, 1 tbsp apple cider vinegar, 1 tbsp Worcestershire sauce, 1 tsp garlic powder, 1 tsp onion powder, salt and pepper to taste.

Directions:

In a saucepan, combine all the ingredients over medium heat. Simmer for 15 minutes, stirring occasionally. Allow the sauce to cool before using. Brush onto your smoked meats during the last 10 minutes of cooking.

Smoky Maple Rub

Ingredients:

2 tbsp smoked paprika, 1 tbsp maple sugar, 1 tbsp brown sugar, 1 tbsp garlic powder, 1 tbsp onion powder, 1 tsp salt, ½ tsp black pepper.

Directions:

In a bowl, mix all the ingredients until well combined. Generously rub onto your meat before smoking. Smoke at a temperature of 225°F for the recommended cooking time.

Honey Sriracha BBQ Sauce

Ingredients:

1 cup ketchup, ½ cup honey, ¼ cup Sriracha sauce, 2 tbsp soy sauce, 1 tbsp apple cider vinegar, 1 tbsp Worcestershire sauce, 1 tsp garlic powder, 1 tsp onion powder, salt and pepper to taste.

Directions:

In a saucepan, combine ketchup, honey, Sriracha sauce, soy sauce, apple cider vinegar, Worcestershire sauce, garlic powder, onion powder, salt, and pepper over medium heat. Simmer for 10 minutes, stirring occasionally. Allow the sauce to cool before using. Brush onto your smoked meats during the last 10 minutes of cooking.

Mango Habanero BBQ Sauce

Ingredients:

1 cup mango puree, ½ cup ketchup, ¼ cup brown sugar, 2 tbsp apple cider vinegar, 1 tbsp Worcestershire sauce, 1 tbsp lime juice, 1 tsp garlic powder, 1 tsp onion powder, 1 habanero pepper (finely chopped), salt and pepper to taste.

Directions:

In a saucepan, combine all the ingredients over medium heat. Simmer for 15 minutes, stirring occasionally. Allow the sauce to cool before using. Brush onto your smoked meats during the last 10 minutes of cooking.

Smoky Garlic Rub

Ingredients:

2 tbsp smoked paprika, 1 tbsp garlic powder, 1 tbsp onion powder, 1 tbsp dried thyme, 1 tbsp dried oregano, 1 tsp salt, ½ tsp black pepper.

Directions:

In a small bowl, combine all the ingredients thoroughly. Rub the mixture generously onto your meat before placing it in the smoker. Smoke at a temperature of 250°F until the meat reaches the desired internal temperature.

Tennessee Whiskey BBQ Sauce

Ingredients:

1 cup ketchup, ½ cup Tennessee whiskey, ¼ cup apple cider vinegar, 2 tbsp brown sugar, 1 tbsp Worcestershire sauce, 1 tbsp molasses, 1 tsp garlic powder, 1 tsp onion powder, salt and pepper to taste.

Directions:

In a saucepan, combine all the ingredients over medium heat. Simmer for 10 minutes, stirring occasionally. Allow the sauce to cool before using. Brush onto your smoked meats during the last 10 minutes of cooking.

Herb-Crusted Rub

Ingredients:

2 tbsp dried parsley, 2 tbsp dried thyme, 1 tbsp dried rosemary, 1 tbsp garlic powder, 1 tbsp onion powder, 1 tsp paprika, 1 tsp salt, ½ tsp black pepper.

Directions:

In a bowl, mix all the ingredients until well combined. Generously rub onto your meat before smoking. Smoke at a temperature of 225°F for the recommended cooking time.

Sweet Teriyaki BBQ Sauce

Ingredients:

1 cup soy sauce, ½ cup brown sugar, ¼ cup honey, 2 tbsp pineapple juice, 1 tbsp apple cider vinegar, 1 tbsp Worcestershire sauce, 1 tsp garlic powder, 1 tsp onion powder, salt and pepper to taste.

Directions:

In a saucepan, combine all the ingredients over medium heat. Simmer for 15 minutes, stirring occasionally. Allow the sauce to cool before using. Brush onto your smoked meats during the last 10 minutes of cooking.

Mexican Spice Rub

Ingredients:

2 tbsp chili powder, 1 tbsp cumin, 1 tbsp paprika, 1 tbsp garlic powder, 1 tbsp onion powder, 1 tsp oregano, 1 tsp salt, ½ tsp black pepper.

Directions:

In a small bowl, combine all the ingredients thoroughly. Rub the mixture generously onto your meat before placing it in the smoker. Smoke at a temperature of 250°F until the meat reaches the desired internal temperature.

Peach Bourbon BBQ Sauce

Ingredients: 1 cup peach preserves, ½ cup ketchup, ¼ cup bourbon, 2 tbsp apple cider vinegar, 1 tbsp Worcestershire sauce, 1 tbsp brown sugar, 1 tsp garlic powder, 1 tsp onion powder, salt and pepper to taste.

Directions: In a saucepan, combine peach preserves, ketchup, bourbon, apple cider vinegar, Worcestershire sauce, brown sugar, garlic powder, onion powder, salt, and pepper over medium heat. Simmer for 10 minutes, stirring occasionally. Allow the sauce to cool before using. Brush onto your smoked meats during the last 10 minutes of cooking.

Lemon Herb Rub

Ingredients:

2 tbsp dried basil, 2 tbsp dried thyme, 1 tbsp dried parsley, 1 tbsp lemon zest, 1 tbsp garlic powder, 1 tbsp onion powder, 1 tsp salt, ½ tsp black pepper.

Directions:

In a small bowl, combine all the ingredients thoroughly. Rub the mixture generously onto your meat before placing it in the smoker. Smoke at a temperature of 250°F until the meat reaches the desired internal temperature.

Smoky Bourbon BBQ Sauce

Ingredients:

1 cup ketchup, ½ cup bourbon, ¼ cup brown sugar, 2 tbsp apple cider vinegar, 1 tbsp Worcestershire sauce, 1 tbsp molasses, 1 tsp garlic powder, 1 tsp onion powder, salt and pepper to taste.

Directions:

In a saucepan, combine all the ingredients over medium heat. Simmer for 10 minutes, stirring occasionally. Allow the sauce to cool before using. Brush onto your smoked meats during the last 10 minutes of cooking.

Jamaican Jerk Rub

Ingredients:

2 tbsp allspice, 1 tbsp dried thyme, 1 tbsp brown sugar, 1 tbsp garlic powder, 1 tbsp onion powder, 1 tsp paprika, 1 tsp cayenne pepper, 1 tsp salt, ½ tsp black pepper.

Directions:

In a bowl, mix all the ingredients until well combined. Generously rub onto your meat before smoking. Smoke at a temperature of 225°F for the recommended cooking time.

Sesame Ginger BBQ Sauce

Ingredients: 1 cup soy sauce, ½ cup brown sugar, ¼ cup rice vinegar, 2 tbsp sesame oil, 1 tbsp minced ginger, 1 tbsp minced garlic, 1 tsp sesame seeds, salt and pepper to taste.

Directions: In a saucepan, combine all the ingredients over medium heat. Simmer for 15 minutes, stirring occasionally. Allow the sauce to cool before using. Brush onto your smoked meats during the last 10 minutes of cooking.

Greek Herb Rub

Ingredients:

2 tbsp dried oregano, 2 tbsp dried thyme, 1 tbsp dried rosemary, 1 tbsp garlic powder, 1 tbsp onion powder, 1 tsp paprika, 1 tsp salt, ½ tsp black pepper.

Directions:

In a small bowl, combine all the ingredients thoroughly. Rub the mixture generously onto your meat before placing it in the smoker. Smoke at a temperature of 250°F until the meat reaches the desired internal temperature.

Asian Barbecue Sauce

Ingredients:

1 cup hoisin sauce, ½ cup soy sauce, ¼ cup honey, 2 tbsp rice vinegar, 1 tbsp minced ginger, 1 tbsp minced garlic, 1 tsp sesame oil, salt and pepper to taste.

Directions:

In a saucepan, combine all the ingredients over medium heat. Simmer for 10 minutes, stirring occasionally. Allow the sauce to cool before using. Brush onto your smoked meats during the last 10 minutes of cooking.

Herb de Provence Rub

Ingredients:

2 tbsp dried thyme, 2 tbsp dried rosemary, 2 tbsp dried marjoram, 1 tbsp dried lavender, 1 tbsp garlic powder, 1 tbsp onion powder, 1 tsp salt, ½ tsp black pepper.

Directions:

In a small bowl, combine all the ingredients thoroughly. Rub the mixture generously onto your meat before placing it in the smoker. Smoke at a temperature of 250°F until the meat reaches the desired internal temperature.

Honey Lime BBQ Sauce

Ingredients:

1 cup ketchup, ½ cup honey, ¼ cup lime juice, 2 tbsp Worcestershire sauce, 1 tbsp soy sauce, 1 tbsp brown sugar, 1 tsp garlic powder, 1 tsp onion powder, salt and pepper to taste.

Directions:

In a saucepan, combine all the ingredients over medium heat. Simmer for 10 minutes, stirring occasionally. Allow the sauce to cool before using. Brush onto your smoked meats during the last 10 minutes of cooking.

Smoky Ranch Rub

Ingredients:

2 tbsp dried parsley, 2 tbsp dried dill, 1 tbsp dried chives, 1 tbsp garlic powder, 1 tbsp onion powder, 1 tsp smoked paprika, 1 tsp salt, ½ tsp black pepper.

Directions:

In a small bowl, combine all the ingredients thoroughly. Rub the mixture generously onto your meat before placing it in the smoker. Smoke at a temperature of 250°F until the meat reaches the desired internal temperature.

Hawaiian BBQ Sauce

Ingredients: 1 cup pineapple juice, ½ cup ketchup, ¼ cup brown sugar, 2 tbsp soy sauce, 1 tbsp apple cider vinegar, 1 tbsp Worcestershire sauce, 1 tsp garlic powder, 1 tsp onion powder, salt and pepper to taste.

Directions: In a saucepan, combine all the ingredients over medium heat. Simmer for 15 minutes, stirring occasionally. Allow the sauce to cool before using. Brush onto your smoked meats during the last 10 minutes of cooking.

Citrus Pepper Rub

Ingredients:

2 tbsp lemon zest, 2 tbsp orange zest, 1 tbsp black pepper, 1 tbsp garlic powder, 1 tbsp onion powder, 1 tsp paprika, 1 tsp salt, ½ tsp cayenne pepper.

Directions:

In a bowl, mix all the ingredients until well combined. Generously rub onto your meat before smoking. Smoke at a temperature of 225°F for the recommended cooking time.

Maple Bacon BBQ Sauce

Ingredients:

1 cup ketchup, ½ cup maple syrup, ¼ cup apple cider vinegar, 2 tbsp Worcestershire sauce, 1 tbsp Dijon mustard, 1 tbsp liquid smoke, 1 tsp garlic powder, 1 tsp onion powder, salt and pepper to taste.

Directions:

In a saucepan, combine all the ingredients over medium heat. Simmer for 10 minutes, stirring occasionally. Allow the sauce to cool before using. Brush onto your smoked meats during the last 10 minutes of cooking.

Southwest Spice Rub

Ingredients:

2 tbsp chili powder, 1 tbsp cumin, 1 tbsp smoked paprika, 1 tbsp garlic powder, 1 tbsp onion powder, 1 tsp oregano, 1 tsp salt, ½ tsp black pepper.

Directions:

In a small bowl, combine all the ingredients thoroughly. Rub the mixture generously onto your meat before placing it in the smoker. Smoke at a temperature of 250°F until the meat reaches the desired internal temperature.

Blackberry Bourbon BBQ Sauce

Ingredients:

1 cup blackberries (fresh or frozen), ½ cup ketchup, ¼ cup bourbon, 2 tbsp apple cider vinegar, 1 tbsp Worcestershire sauce, 1 tbsp brown sugar, 1 tsp garlic powder, 1 tsp onion powder, salt and pepper to taste.

Directions:

In a saucepan, combine all the ingredients over medium heat. Simmer for 15 minutes, stirring occasionally and crushing the blackberries. Allow the sauce to

Sweet Thai Chili BBQ Sauce

Ingredients:

1 cup sweet chili sauce, ½ cup ketchup, ¼ cup soy sauce, 2 tbsp rice vinegar, 1 tbsp brown sugar, 1 tbsp minced garlic, 1 tbsp minced ginger, salt and pepper to taste.

Directions:

In a saucepan, combine all the ingredients over medium heat. Simmer for 10 minutes, stirring occasionally. Allow the sauce to cool before using. Brush onto your smoked meats during the last 10 minutes of cooking.

Moroccan Spice Rub

Ingredients:

2 tbsp ground cumin, 2 tbsp ground coriander, 1 tbsp paprika, 1 tbsp ground ginger, 1 tbsp ground cinnamon, 1 tbsp garlic powder, 1 tbsp onion powder, 1 tsp cayenne pepper, 1 tsp salt.

Directions:

In a small bowl, combine all the ingredients thoroughly. Rub the mixture generously onto your meat before placing it in the smoker. Smoke at a temperature of 250°F until the meat reaches the desired internal temperature.

Pineapple Ginger BBQ Sauce

Ingredients:

1 cup pineapple juice, ½ cup ketchup, ¼ cup brown sugar, 2 tbsp soy sauce, 1 tbsp apple cider vinegar, 1 tbsp Worcestershire sauce, 1 tbsp minced ginger, 1 tsp garlic powder, salt and pepper to taste.

Directions:

In a saucepan, combine all the ingredients over medium heat. Simmer for 15 minutes, stirring occasionally. Allow the sauce to cool before using. Brush onto your smoked meats during the last 10 minutes of cooking.

Smokey Southwest Rub

Ingredients:

2 tbsp smoked paprika, 1 tbsp chili powder, 1 tbsp cumin, 1 tbsp garlic powder, 1 tbsp onion powder, 1 tsp oregano, 1 tsp salt, ½ tsp black pepper.

Directions:

In a small bowl, combine all the ingredients thoroughly. Rub the mixture generously onto your meat before placing it in the smoker. Smoke at a temperature of 250°F until the meat reaches the desired internal temperature.

Honey Dijon BBQ Sauce

Ingredients:

1 cup Dijon mustard, ½ cup honey, ¼ cup apple cider vinegar, 2 tbsp Worcestershire sauce, 1 tbsp soy sauce, 1 tbsp brown sugar, 1 tsp garlic powder, 1 tsp onion powder, salt and pepper to taste.

Directions:

In a saucepan, combine all the ingredients over medium heat. Simmer for 10 minutes, stirring occasionally. Allow the sauce to cool before using. Brush onto your smoked meats during the last 10 minutes of cooking.

COOKING CHART ELECTRIC SMOKER

The Grillfather	Smoking Temp	Finished Temp	Smoking Time
Brisket	225°F (107°C)	195°F (90°C)	1 hour per pound
Tri-Tip	225°F (107°C)	130-135°F (55-57°C)	2 - 3 hours
Ribeye Steak	225°F (107°C)	130-135°F (55-57°C)	1 - 2 hours
Short Ribs	225°F (107°C)	200-205°F (93-96°C)	4 - 5 hours
Tenderloin	225°F (107°C)	130-135°F (55-57°C)	1 - 2 hours
Chicken (whole)	225°F (107°C)	165°F (74°C)	3 - 4 hours
Turkey (whole)	275°F (135°C)	165°F (74°C)	4 - 5 hours
Duck Breast	225°F (107°C)	155°F (68°C)	1 - 1.5 hours

The Grillfather

		Smoking Temp	Finished Temp	Smoking Time
	Cornish Hen	225°F (107°C)	165°F (74°C)	2 - 3 hours
	Rack of Lamb	225°F (107°C)	130-135°F (55-57°C)	2 - 3 hours
	Leg of Lamb	225°F (107°C)	145°F (63°C)	2 - 3 hours
	Lamb Chops	225°F (107°C)	130-135°F (55-57°C)	57°C) 1 - 2 hours
	Ground Lamb (Kofta)	225°F (107°C)	160°F (71°C)	1 - 1.5 hours
	Pulled Pork	225°F (107°C)	195°F (90°C)	1.5 - 2 hours per pound
	Pork Ribs	225°F (107°C)	195°F (90°C)	4 - 5 hours

The Grillfather

	Smoking Temp	Finished Temp	Smoking Time
Tuna	225°F (107°C)	130-140°F (55-60°C)	30 - 45 minutes
Lobster Tails	225°F (107°C)	140-145°F (60-63°C)	1 - 1.5 hours
Crab Legs	225°F (107°C)	140-145°F (60-63°C)	1 - 1.5 hours
Bell Peppers	225°F (107°C)	N/A	30 - 45 minutes
Zucchini	225°F (107°C)	N/A	20 - 30 minutes
Eggplant	225°F (107°C)	N/A	30 - 45 minutes
Portobello Mushrooms	225°F (107°C)	N/A	20 - 30 minutes

A Gift for You!!!

HELLO AND THANK YOU
FOR PURCHASING THE BOOK!
I HAVE PREPARED A **NICE SURPRISE FOR YOU**
TO GET THE MOST OUT OF YOUR BBQ.
YOU WILL TOTALLY SURPRISE YOUR FAMILY AND FRIENDS
THANKS TO THESE USEFUL TIPS.
SCAN THE QR CODE NOW
AND FIND OUT WHAT IT'S ALL ABOUT

Made in the USA
Monee, IL
30 July 2023

40164406R00063